T0147529

THE COLLECTIVE WORKS OF
JAIME ALVAREZ

FEATURING
"Dichos de Mi Madre"

—

"Sayings of My Mother"

Jaime Alvarez

authorHOUSE®

AuthorHouse™
1663 Liberty Drive
Bloomington, IN 47403
www.authorhouse.com
Phone: 1-800-839-8640

Published by AuthorHouse   11/26/2012

ISBN: 978-1-4772-8872-6 (sc)
ISBN: 978-1-4772-8871-9 (e)

Library of Congress Control Number: 2012921243

Any people depicted in stock imagery provided by Thinkstock are models, and such images are being used for illustrative purposes only. Certain stock imagery © Thinkstock.

This book is printed on acid-free paper.

The proverbs of Solomon the son of David, the king of Israel, for one to know wisdom and discipline, to discern the sayings of understanding, to receive the discipline that gives insight, righteousness, to give to the inexperienced ones shrewdness, to a young man knowledge and thinking ability —

Proverbs 1:1-4

Dedication

This book is dedicated to my wife, Eunice; and my daughters, Leticia, Marisela, Elena, and Gina; my son-in-law's, Victor Labastida, Hector Labastida, John Eastland and my grandchildren, Jenaru V. Mion, Jasmine Eastland, John Jaime Eastland, Priscila Merriman, Hector Labastida Jr., Katrina Labastida, Isaac Labastida, Leonardo Labastida, Victor Labastida Jr., Seth Labastida, Ivana Bosch, Vivian Bosch, and last but never least Sophia Bosch; my brother-in-law, Reuben Vizcarra; additionally to my beloved friends and my special secret friend that will stay anonymous.

They say to save the best for last. I make a super special dedication to my beloved mother, Elena Alvarez, who is my hero.

Contents

Introduction

The Collective Works of Jaime Alvarez
Featuring Dichos de Mi Madre

My works consist of sayings, poems, and true short stories that I have accumulated throughout my 62 years of life. Some sayings are of my own origin while others are touchstones I have learned from others. My mother, Elena Alvarez, played a prominent role in my life. That is why I commenced my book with "Dichos de Mi Madre," which means, "Sayings of My Mother." The poems and stories are mine.

I intended to provide life lessons in all of them. In life there's only one thing you cannot teach, and that is experience. My goal is to share some of my personal experiences and beliefs with loved ones, especially young people.

It has been said that there is nothing new under the sun. I do not believe that history repeats itself, but people do! My greatest wish is that people who read, My Collective Works, will find meaning in the lessons and apply them in their own lives.

My Purpose for Writing This Book

An old and dying Rabbi was asked if he feared death. He answered that it was not death he feared rather it was becoming irrelevant and forgotten that was his fear. I too want to be remembered by those I love even when I fall asleep in death. If a father, mother, grandfather, grandmother, daughter, son, grandchild, or friend reads or repeats one of these sayings, I still live. This book is meant to be part of my legacy.

Some of the true life experiences will touch loved ones in different ways. The important thing is that I will continue to touch them in a positive way. Unlike my father who regretted the way he lived his life on his deathbed, I want to be able to smile and be very thankful on mine.

Even the picture on the cover of this book is very special to me. In SKIN FOR SKIN, my first book, the picture on the cover shows a warrior capable of doing anything necessary to protect his family. It is a picture that captures the anger and fear of a father who knows evil people are trying to hurt his family.

The picture on the cover of this book shows the real me. The steamboat round roast was our gift to our daughter's, Leticia and Marisela, on their 25th wedding anniversary. John Eastland is Leticia's husband and Hector Labastida Is Marisela's husband. My wife Eunice, a dear friend Teri and I fed approximately 200 guests at our daughter's anniversary dinner. It took over nine hours to fully cook that 80 pound prime hind roast. At the end of the evening I was very tired but very satisfied. It was the spiritual and emotional satisfaction that can only come from serving others and doing it free. There truly is much more joy in giving than receiving. Through it all I have relished the opportunity of being the chef. In French, chef means, "CHIEF!"

Jaime Alvarez

Dichos de Mi Madre

—

Sayings of My Mother

My beautiful Mother Elena and I

ON LIFE

Spanish   *Es mejor volverse colorado una vez que volverse colorado cien veces.*

English   *It is better to turn red one time versus turning red 100 times.*

LIFE LESSON

Have you ever had someone or a circumstance bothering you? Avoiding a civilized confrontation only makes matters worse because of the constant irritation. Handle it now! Sometimes that requires a simple no. Do not carry grudges.

ON LIFE

Spanish   *El ladron se entrega porque corre y se esconde.*

English   *The thief identifies himself because he runs and hides.*

LIFE LESSON

A person's conduct will reveal their nefarious intentions. An honest person does not run and hide. With life experience we learn to rely on what people DO not necessarily what they SAY.

ON LIFE

Spanish   *Candelario de la calle, oscuridad de su casa.*

English   *Candelabra (Light) of the street but darkness of their house.*

LIFE LESSON

Good deeds begin at home with family not with strangers. A truly decent person takes care of their OWN first!

ON LIFE

Spanish   *El diablo es mas diablo por viejo que por diablo.*

English   *The devil is more a devil because of his age rather than because he is a devil.*

LIFE LESSON

There should be a positive accumulated wisdom by sheer experience that comes with age. Unfortunately that is not always the case.

ON LIFE

Spanish   *Arranque de caballo, parar de burro.*

English   *The start of a race horse, the stopping of a donkey.*

LIFE LESSON

Have you ever known a person that is always starting something but never seems to finish or complete the project? Life is not a sprint but a steady trot. The end of the matter, or shall we say, the finished product is what counts.

Some people might be a little manic when starting, like a race horse that bursts out of the gate. Then, like a donkey, they stop and it is almost impossible to get a donkey moving when it decides to stop.

ON LIFE

Spanish   *El hacerle un favor a un ingrato es insultarlo.*

English   *To do a favor for an ingrate is to insult them.*

LIFE LESSON

Some people are ingrates. They are takers and not givers. We can have the best intentions when we try and help them, but it always seems to turn out wrong. Ingrates seem to find a way to make themselves the victim.

Some of us tend to be rescuers and try our best to help others. In most cases the rescuer becomes the persecutor, especially if there are expectations, of the ingrate. Remember a scorpion will always be a scorpion.

ON LIFE

Spanish   *No se puede tapar el sol con un solo dedo.*

English   *You cannot cover the sun with a finger.*

LIFE LESSON

Denial is very destructive. Some acts or conduct are obviously wrong and in too many cases some people want to not say anything or try and hide the wrong. I call this the "CODE OF SILENCE." Some families live by this unwritten code. The truth is everybody probably knows what's going on. Our best efforts cannot cover the sun's brightness with one finger.

ON LIFE

Spanish   *Los niños y los borrachos dicen lo que sienten.*

English   *Children and drunks tell the truth about what they feel.*

LIFE LESSON

Children tend to be honest. Drunks are usually very weak individuals who carry a lot of resentment because of the choices they made in their lives. They do not take responsibility and they consider themselves the VICTIM. They lash out when their inhibitions are removed due to alcohol or some other drug.

Life is about deposits and withdrawals and we are all responsible for what we say. Sometimes their "I'm sorry" becomes diluted because it has been worn out. Children lack emotional maturity so they insist on doing what they feel; this is what makes them children. Drunks have no excuse, in my opinion.

ON LIFE

Spanish   *El que no mira adelante se queda atras.*

English   *The one that does not look ahead will be left behind.*

LIFE LESSON

All our choices have consequences, for good or for bad. Sometimes bad choices are like spitting into the wind. It will probably come back and hit us in the face. There are many good lessons and sayings on this matter. For example "the one who does not plan, plans to fail." We live in the present and plan for the future. Life's law of consequences is that, "you reap what you sow." Life teaches us about the law of consequences. Like it or not we all "reap what we sow."

ON LIFE

Spanish   *Tiene mas excusas que un saco roto.*

English   *He has more excuses than a torn gunny sack.*

LIFE LESSON

There is another saying that states, "Excuses don't put money in the bank." There are times we cannot fulfill an obligation, this happens to all of us. It is important to avoid becoming a chronic excuse maker or blamer. What is inexcusable is always making excuses.

IN JULY 2012, MY BELOVED MOTHER WAS DIAGNOSED WITH ALZHEIMER'S DISEASE. IT MAKES KEEPING HER SAYINGS ALIVE OF EVEN MORE IMPORTANCE.

Sayings on Life
and
Lessons to Live By

Some sayings are of my own origin others are touchstones I have picked up along my journey. Since history does not repeat itself, but people do, I sincerely hope you find some of them useful. Our young people need nuggets of wisdom to help navigate the complicated world we live in. When you read this book, share some of the sayings with loved ones and friends. Try to inculcate the meaning in their hearts.

ON LIFE

Life is full of paradoxes. Happiness comes when you realize it is not only about YOU! There is truly more joy in giving than receiving. The Bible says that to give one's life to save another is the greatest love a human being can display. That does not always mean dying.

LIFE LESSON

If a person gained all the riches and fame in the world but is unhappy, of what value would all the riches be? True happiness is internal and spiritual, not external and carnal. Every day we should do something that brings happiness to ourselves and others.

ON LIFE

May your passion become your righteous mission.

LIFE LESSON

Passion is the fuel that drives our mission. If you have passion for what you are doing, you will succeed at anything. Passion is an intense enthusiasm for something. We all should have goals. Make them your passion no matter how old you are.

ON LIFE

God has given all of us gifts. If you do not use your gift, you will not be "true to thine own self." It could become your life curse.

LIFE LESSON

I believe we are all blessed with certain gifts from God. Some of these are innate. If you develop your gifts whether it is singing, writing, mechanics, public speaking, whatever your gift may be, and then you can be "true to thine own self". If you do not develop your gifts, one day you will say, "I could have been this or I should have been that." You can be sure of one thing; you will never do it, if you don't try! Remember, everything you do, do it for the glory and honor of your God. Try to fulfill your God given potential, only you can.

ON LIFE

I do not believe in good or bad luck but I do believe in good and bad energy.

LIFE LESSON

Luck is supposedly good or bad things that happen by chance. Personally I do not believe things happen by chance for good or for bad. Our choices produce the energy and vitality required to succeed or fail.

ON LIFE

I will trust a spiritual person more than a religious one.

LIFE LESSON

Sometimes religious individuals can be fanatically blinded by their prejudice. Especially when they believe that only they are right. Islamic extremists, for example, will kill men, women and children that they believe to be infidels. There is no doubt they are extremely religious and believe they are doing the right thing. A spiritual person is not a threat but rather a loving and kind individual, that is because they see their God as benevolent and not punitive. Some very special people can be both religious and spiritual. That would be the best of all worlds.

ON LIFE

My greatest realization and liberation is to accept the fact that I am only human.

LIFE LESSON

Never take yourself so seriously that you forget the fact that you are an imperfect human being. We all make mistakes, that is the human experience. Embrace your humanity and enjoy life and those you love.

ON LIFE

Assumption is the mother of disaster.

LIFE LESSON

How many times have we thought something was going to be a certain way and it was not? Assumption can lead to discord and confusion. Communicate and clarify matters, twice if you have to, and avoid disaster. Do not trick yourself into hearing and believing what you want to hear and believe.

ON LIFE

Not even the greatest pitcher in the major leagues can throw a curveball like life can.

LIFE LESSON

When I was a young man I played a lot of baseball. There are valuable life lessons in sports. In baseball when you are batting, you are taught to expect a fastball and if it is over the plate you can hit it. Sometimes the pitcher fools you by throwing a slow breaking curveball, low and outside.

Life also throws you many curveballs. A good hitter is able to adjust by keeping his eye on the ball.

ON LIFE

A hero is defined by the adversity he overcomes in defense of others

LIFE LESSON

We can be heroes every day. It doesn't have to be a life or death situation. Doing the right thing should become an important part of our character. Strive to do the right thing. Doing the right thing should become a constant and you can trust that which is constant. Defending the innocent and downtrodden is as heroic as it gets.

ON LIFE

Nobody can escape the law of consequence.

LIFE LESSON

For every action there is a reaction, for good or for bad. Good choices usually produce good consequences. We always have the power of choice.

ON LIFE

In business the hardest question to answer is, "what is your business?" In life we should question "what is my purpose?"

LIFE LESSON

In my life I have observed people who have no purpose but to exist. That is not truly living. Know who you are and that you are special and unique. There is no other YOU in the world. Define your purpose in your life and thrive. Remember true life is not a means to an end but an end to a means.

ON LIFE

Resiliency and reinvention are two of life's favorite children.

LIFE LESSON

A resilient person is able to recover quickly from difficult situations. Sometimes in our personal journey through life, reinventing ourselves is a must. Reinvention could be a new career, a lifestyle change, such as relocation, or other challenges. Aging requires resiliency and reinvention! Learn to be flexible and see reinventing oneself for what it really is, a new adventure.

ON LIFE

There is a great difference between asking for courage and strength, and then having the courage to use it.

LIFE LESSON

The question sometimes is not, what should I do? But will I have the courage to do it!? Excuses are habit-forming. We must be able to take responsibility for our choices. Walt Disney said that when he had an idea, he would purposely ask 10 people their opinion. When 10 people would express doubt or negativity he knew it was a good idea. When we feel strongly about doing something, and have done our due diligence, we must have the courage and strength to go forward. Of course this includes a written plan. Avoid sins of omission and do not be cowardly.

ON LIFE

The worst deceit is self-deceit because the deceiver is always with you.

LIFE LESSON

Honesty starts with one's self. If we are deceiving ourselves about choices we make, or intend to make, the deceiver is always with us. We cannot escape ourselves.

Sometimes we can become our worst enemy because we want to believe our own lies. Eventually our self-deception will cause our own ruinous fall.

ON LIFE

You can trust that which is constant and true.

LIFE LESSON

God's universe is constant. We can trust that our sun will rise in the morning and bring a new day. As humans we should strive to be as constant and trustworthy as possible. If we give our word that we will do something, make sure you follow through. People who are inconsistent cannot be depended upon or trusted.

ON LIFE

One of the secrets to a happy life is never taking your blessings for granted.

LIFE LESSON

Happiness is the ultimate goal of our lives. True happiness requires that we be conscious of the many blessings we have. Happiness is also a choice! It is not a gift, but rather something we must build. Gratitude is the foundation of happiness. Our relationship with loved ones is precious and should be safeguarded. Fools do not appreciate their blessings until they lose them. They then look back with regret.

ON LIFE

Blindly following man's rules does not teach you the difference between right and wrong it just makes you ignorant and proud.

LIFE LESSON

Some people are too ready to give up their thinking ability and personal responsibility. It is much easier to follow man's rules when it comes to religion and politics. That relieves them of the challenge of having to think for oneself. We must develop a healthy conscience and relationship with our God. Men tend to be manipulative and self-serving. We as individuals must develop our own moral compass of what is right or wrong. As we mature spiritually and physically, we should become less credulous. We should not be ready to believe theory or dogma without careful examination. In the 1960s, the leader of China, Mao Tse Tung, when asked, "how do you control the masses?," responded, "keep them ignorant".

ON LIFE

In most cases the first step to mental health is forgiving our parents.

LIFE LESSON

Almost all of us have suffered some type of abuse or mistreatment when growing up, some more than others. In some cases it is necessary to forgive our parents for their flaws and mistakes they made when raising us. Perhaps they were doing their best with the tools they were given.

The only way to try and rectify the past is by us becoming better human beings. We should make the choice of becoming good spouses and parents. We did not ask to be born into a certain family. We had no choice in the matter! But we certainly have the power and responsibility when we become the parents and grandparents to break the MOLD if necessary!

ON LIFE

Excuses are a sign of a person's weakness. Let your yes be yes and your no be no, whenever possible!

LIFE LESSON

We are all creatures of habit. These habits whether good or bad are learned behavior. Whenever possible when you say you will do something follow through on your word. Make your word valuable by being reliable. Sometimes it is better to say a polite NO rather than a false YES! Do not place yourself in a position of having to constantly make excuses or apologies. Excuses never accomplished anything and dilute your character.

ON LIFE

There are always more opportunities than there is time or money.

LIFE LESSON

Being fragmented is a sure path to becoming ineffective. Choose what you decide to pursue wisely and don't make hasty decisions. Your time is your friend not your slave. Your time is precious and you should cherish and nurture it.

ON LIFE

You cannot lose something you never had.

LIFE LESSON

Sometimes we convince ourselves that we absolutely must have something. Life rarely turns out the way we plan. When something material cannot be attained, for any reason, there is no need to fret.

Your life will continue and your happiness should not depend on material items. It is easy to replace an object of your desire with something else. There is no real loss if you never had it.

ON LIFE

A headcount revealed that there are more horse rears in the world than there are horses.

LIFE LESSON

Do not wear your feelings on your sleeve. It is inevitable that we will encounter rude individuals; just remember that this person is probably one of the horse rears that is just not attached to a horse.

ON LIFE

Make your great memories today.

LIFE LESSON

In the end of the matter, we are left with our memories. Like a computer, our mind stores and remembers events and information. People and places make up our memory. We can influence those futuristic remembrances by creating them today. Always strive to be a decent human being and most of your memories will be happy ones.

ON LIFE

You are never too old to create something that benefits your loved ones. Good deeds elevate people's spirits. Even a simple smile can reassure a person. Plus, it makes you look more beautiful or handsome.

LIFE LESSON

My daughter Elena, who is a marriage and family therapist, taught me that negativity is approximately seven times more powerful than positivity. Negativity is an emotional vampire that can drain our best intentions. Strive to be a positive uplifting person whenever possible. It really is your CHOICE.

ON LIFE

Drink to remember and not to forget.

LIFE LESSON

I love beer. Usually when I drink it is with my wife. She enjoys drinking Chardonnay wine. We take advantage of this opportunity to remember the many experiences of our lives, especially our youth. Some memories are very personal and only belong to us. We drink our wine and our beer with no regrets.

ON LIFE

You can understand the dead not communicating; but certainly not the living.

LIFE LESSON

Communicate, communicate, and communicate! So many misunderstandings could be avoided if a person makes a good habit of always communicating. Especially professional people should always communicate with their clients. This avoids a tremendous amount of anxiety.

ON LIFE

Slander attempts to destroy everything in a person's past, present, and future.

LIFE LESSON

Slander is making a false and damaging statement about someone. As a person gets older, and a little wiser, you learn that giving people the benefit of the doubt is a smart thing to do. Be careful to not repeat potential falsehoods about someone. The damage could be irreparable. Avoid absolutes.

ON LIFE

We are the architects of our own destiny.

LIFE LESSON

We are the sum total of our experiences and our choices. For good or for bad we are our own architects. Sometimes we hold ourselves back out of fear. It is up to us and us alone to fulfill our destiny.

ON LIFE

What others think of us should not define who we really are.

LIFE LESSON

With age, you realize that it is impossible to please everybody. Some people are not going to like us and that's a fact. Be sure of who you are and what you stand for. Try and respect everyone but understand that they do not define your meaning.

ON LIFE

Avoid conflict whenever possible but if there is no alternative, pray for the dead and fight like hell for the living.

LIFE LESSON

There is always collateral damage when there is a war of any kind. Do everything in your power to avoid the cost of battle. When all peaceable efforts have been exhausted, and you are forced into battle, fight to win as quickly as possible.

ON LIFE

Winning your enemies over is destroying them.

LIFE LESSON

When I was growing up in the 60s, in El Monte, California, there was a great deal of hate between some Mexican and white students. The Mexicans were known as "cholos" and the white students were called "surfers or patties." Fights often broke out between these two groups. In many ways they considered each other enemies. A very smart coach decided to create lunch meetings between the leaders of the rival groups. It wasn't long before they came to realize that they had more in common than they ever imagined. In high school most boys like girls, music, cars and sports. The wise coach was able to apply the concept of destroying your perceived enemies by winning them over. To win a war without firing a single shot or harming someone is the greatest victory of all.

ON LIFE

"When in hell, keep going." Winston Churchill

LIFE LESSON

Sometimes in our lives, it truly seems that there is no way out of a situation. The English people experienced potential annihilation by Adolf Hitler's Nazi war machine during World War II.

Winston Churchill rallied the nation by elevating their fighting spirit and they became unconquerable. When we feel that we are in hell, what should we do? Keep going! Throughout my family's struggle, I would remind myself, "this too shall pass."

ON LIFE

Things are never as bad as they seem when you face up to them.

LIFE LESSON

I have lived by this saying my entire life. When we avoid a problem it doesn't always go away. Sometimes more negative energy is created by avoidance than strategic confrontation. If we tried to ignore a pressing issue, we tend to internalize it. The problem or situation can consume us. The interesting consequence is that if you face up to the challenge it probably isn't as terrible as you thought. Try it!

ON LIFE

When people talk of justice we must ask the question, "Whose justice are we talking about?"

LIFE LESSON

Justice is treatment that is right and fair. Early in life you should learn that life sometimes is not fair. History teaches this fact clearly. We as individuals can strive to be just persons. It is only this justice that we have control over.

ON LIFE

May you strive for insight and understanding in your personal journey and avoid the destructive nature of foolishness.

LIFE LESSON

For good or for bad, we all reap the consequences of our choices and actions. A wise person looks around and studies the behavior of others, not with the intention of judging, but in order to gain insight. There are good examples we can emulate and there are bad examples which teach us what to avoid. The Bible is a great source of insight and understanding.

The Bible is full of stories of those who lived and died. Their personal failures and triumphs are revealed in order for us to learn about life. Some of their conduct was despicable and merits being discussed even if they are dead. This also applies today to relatives or those we were perhaps close to. How can we understand light if we have never seen darkness? The consequences and finality of their choices will help guide us to avoid foolishness. It is wise to teach our children the difference between good and bad, not only in words, but more importantly by example. Our children when they are young usually do not know what they will be when they grow up. It is probably more important for them to know what they will NOT become!

ON LIFE

Stop trying to tell God what to do!

LIFE LESSON

It has been my personal experience that some circumstances that I stubbornly wanted to maintain or accomplish were not in my best interest. Now that I look back at 62 years old, I realize that God had a better plan. I just could not see it.

Some things cannot be spoken of in advance, but God knows. I personally have made a conscious choice to stop trying to tell God what to do!

ON LIFE

When someone feels sorry for themselves and says, "NOBODY LOVES ME," you have to wonder when was the last time THEY loved somebody?

LIFE LESSON

I emphasize the need for personal responsibility. We do become the sum total of our choices and experiences. Some people work very hard to be victims by choice. They will often say, "NOBODY LOVES ME." In life there tends to be takers and givers. Love must be given away in order to receive it. Victims marinate in their self-pity. That is why many people become "islands." It is important for us to show our love by giving of ourselves and sometimes that's unconditional.

ON LIFE

Jealousy is like a bull running wild in a china shop.

LIFE LESSON

Resentment is the evil child born of jealousy. Its destructive power knows no boundaries. Like a wild bull running loose in a china shop, it destroys everything in its path. Some of the valuable china that it breaks cannot ever be replaced. The wounds inflicted can scar, but some may not really heal. A jealous person's memory can be of perpetual existence and re-live events as if they were happening that very moment. Nobody can be happy or make someone else happy if jealousy is present. Jealousy and insecurity go hand-in-hand.

ON LIFE

Some things cannot be spoken of in advance.

LIFE LESSON

It is a mistake to be overly confident about results not revealed. Even the utilizing of great effort does not assure the outcome of a matter. When inspiration and opportunity present themselves, your effort should be shrouded in modesty. In this manner you will avoid appearing foolish.

ON LIFE

We are creatures of habit and for that reason we should be careful what we choose to practice.

LIFE LESSON

There are good and bad habits. Bad habits seem to come more naturally than good habits, to some of us. If not tempered, we will become our habit. For example, one who over drinks frequently will probably become a drunk. Likewise, the one who tells many lies will become a liar. We must practice good habits daily. Good habits are learned and are maintained through consistency.

ON LIFE

There are very few things we can really control in our life perhaps the most important one is keeping our word.

LIFE LESSON

Once we give our word that we will do something we are morally obligated. People will respect and admire a person that keeps their word. It is very sad to see a person that is flaky, which means not trustworthy. Once that label has been earned, unfortunately, a lifetime may not make it disappear.

Keeping your word is a moral choice. We have full control over it in most cases. Morality has to do with knowing the difference between right and wrong.

ON LIFE

In most cases, the question is not what should I do? But rather, will I do it?

LIFE LESSON

Emotional maturity requires us to take responsibility for our actions. In many cases we know the difference between right and wrong. Sometimes we will try and rationalize why we can't do something or why we should do something. Develop and listen to your inner voice which is your conscience. Train yourself to do the right thing and don't spend a lot of time rationalizing in an effort to convince yourself to do what is wrong. You always have the power of choice. It might sound simplistic but just do it!

ON LIFE

Even a stopped clock is right twice a day.

LIFE LESSON

Don't discard what people have to say. A wise person listens and digests information. Sometimes the answer you are looking for can come from the most unlikely source.

ON LIFE

Sometimes a cigar is just a cigar and not a phallic symbol.

LIFE LESSON

Our perception is our reality. We must be careful not to over think matters and create an erroneous idea in our minds. Be careful to not readily impugn a person's character or intent as cynical people tend to do.

ON LIFE

Our morality is what separates us from the animal world. Spirituality is a basic need in our lives, it must be fed or it dies.

LIFE LESSON

Animals are guided by instinct. Survival is the only thing that matters for them. You might say that animals truly live by the law of survival of the fittest. The beautiful and seemingly loving mother lioness would not hesitate in killing the mother leopard's baby cubs given a chance. Most animals will mate with any other animal of its kind when in season. There are exceptions, of course. Our moral values elevate us above wild animals. I have seen so many lives hurt and destroyed by lack of impulse control. Protect and nourish you mind, body, and soul.

ON LIFE

The dear that runs and leaps so gracefully in the forest should not criticize the ox that toils in the farmer's field.

LIFE LESSON

We should not expect others to think and act the way we do. Respect the fact that everybody is an individual with different God given traits and abilities. Our diversity serves a divine purpose and is not contingent upon our limited time and space.

ON LIFE

Any human can inherit unsolicited circumstances that can instantly change our fragile lives. We all have our turn in life's tumbler.

LIFE LESSON

There are no guarantees in life and sometimes life is unfair. Unforeseen circumstances befall all of us. Make it your goal to not allow yourself to embrace victimhood. True champions pick themselves up many times, if necessary. This is why they are champions.

ON LIFE

Powerlifting is power versus mass. When bench pressing, you must keep the loaded bar moving upwards. Not only are you battling the heavyweight but gravity as well. If you stop pressing the weight, it can come back and crush you.

LIFE LESSON

Not giving up is an essential part of successful living. Keep pressing forward, even if it is slowly. Even if you are taking baby steps you are still moving forward. When possible, prepare yourself for challenges, both solicited and unsolicited. Your spiritual and physical preparation will allow you to succeed. Your mind is the most powerful tool you possess. Exercise it diligently.

Jaime Alvarez, Masters Bench Press Champion,
54 to 60 year old division at 181lbs.

ON LIFE

In power-lifting the way you gain strength is to reach failure.

LIFE LESSON

When I was helping people gain strength in their bench-press, they would be surprised when I would tell them to bench until failure. What I meant was to load the bar with a little more weight than they could actually press. A spotter could help them raise the bar. This method would allow their brain and body to accustom itself to the weight. In strength training FAILURE is not a bad thing necessarily. In life, we can all learn from our failures and improve ourselves. People's fear of failure will prevent them from doing great things. Strive for excellence. Your failures are stepping stones that eventually will lead you to your goal.

ON LIFE

Relative thinking helps you understand that life has not targeted you for special pain. You must always remember that there are so many other people in much more difficult and even dire circumstances.

LIFE LESSON

When a person starts feeling sorry for him or herself they should go visit a Children's Cancer Center or a Veterans hospital and see how they can help. It is offensive to heaven and earth when one only thinks of themselves.

ON LIFE

I believe that little children are the closest thing to angels on this earth. Does that make loving mothers the closest thing to God?

LIFE LESSON

The Bible says that God is love. There is no greater love, born of humans, than a mother's love for her child. Even at a young age, I have always favored the women in my life. It started with my relationship with my mother. She was always a loving constant in my life, my father was not. I praise all women who are blessed mothers. Almighty God knew exactly what he was doing when he gave women the gift of life.

ON LIFE

When you are in serious trouble, whether solicited or not, take the opportunity to find out who your real friends are.

LIFE LESSON

In reality we have very few real friends. During a crisis true friends will reveal themselves. They will stand by your side come hell or high water. There will be many acquaintances but a friend is a very special person. Through the fog of war your true friends will be revealed. Take names and never forget who your real friends are.

ON LIFE

It has been said that money has wings. It seems that my money not only has wings but also a turbo charged jet engine that makes it fly away in the blink of an eye.

LIFE LESSON

The Bible says, "The love of money is the root of all evil." Notice that it does not say that money itself is the root of all evil. If a person puts all their faith and trust in money it can be dangerous and faulty thinking. I have always been amazed at how quickly money can be lost, in the blink of an eye it seems. Even investing in real estate or the stock market is a risk. Fortunes are made but more are lost. Anchor your trust in spiritual matters, and remember "HEALTH IS WEALTH."

ON LIFE

There are some people that light up the room when they walk in and there are people who cause the room to light up when they leave.

LIFE LESSON

We all create and carry with us a certain type of energy. Positive people that care about others are a needed and welcomed source of warmth and light. It has been estimated that negativity is seven times more powerful than positivity. Think about how drained you feel after being with a negative person. They are like emotional vampires. They are powerful but not in an uplifting way. Avoid negative people and surround yourself with positive ones. You will be much happier.

ON LIFE

Be wary of people who say, "Don't tell anyone. You are the only one I will say this to," or "trust me," too often.

LIFE LESSON

I have observed that some people use these admonitions frequently. More than likely they have requested the same from others. It is similar and related to the principal that if someone is constantly gossiping about others they are probably gossiping about you. Those who repeatedly say "trust me" are usually trying to win an argument or control someone. If you have developed a reputation of being honest and truthful, the words "trust me" are not necessary.

ON LIFE

"There are two types of people in this world, the decent and the indecent"-Dr. Victor Frankel

LIFE LESSON

This was Dr. Victor Frankel's conclusion about people after suffering years of torture in the Nazi concentration camp known as Auschwitz. During his years of enslavement, Dr. Frankel, witnessed many atrocities, injustices and death. Even in that horrible environment there were acts of benevolence on the part of decent people. It sounds like a simple statement but that is the conclusion this great man's observations brought him to. We should all strive to be decent people and do the right thing. Remember what Dr. Victor Frankel taught the world, "BETWEEN STIMULI AND REACTION, there's always CHOICE."

ON LIFE

"Make your friends before you need them." I believe this was said in the movie THE GODFATHER.

LIFE LESSON

It has been my experience that politics exist in all of man's endeavors. That is not necessarily a bad or corrupt situation. I have had the privilege of knowing some very decent and powerful people. With that said, I have also never given up my thinking ability and have always tried to recognize people for who they really are. The exceptional and special people I wanted to befriend, never expecting anything in return, but their friendship. In conjunction with the saying of "make your friends before you need them", it should be said, "hope you never need to impose on them." Always be a true friend and be willing to help those special people you call friends even if it is just a word of encouragement.

ON LIFE

The answers to life's challenges are usually right in front of us if we have the courage to open our eyes.

LIFE LESSON

Sometimes we complicate matters by over thinking things. It sometimes requires great courage to do what is right. That is what having character is all about. Learn to see the obvious by not trying to rationalize or excuse matters of importance. Keep things simple whenever possible.

ON LIFE

Life is fair… it beats everybody up!

LIFE LESSON

It is important for us to understand that everybody has problems. Life is hard. The healthy point of view is to not consider ourselves constant victims. Do not allow yourself to wallow in self-pity, always asking "why does everything bad happen to me?" Everything in life is relative and the struggle never ends until we fall asleep in death. Dr. Scott Peck said, "Life is hard, once you accept that fact it is not so hard."

ON LIFE

Do not be afraid to look squarely in the eyes of adversity. Embrace the challenge. It is usually what we do not see or refuse to acknowledge that causes us harm.

LIFE LESSON

We all face adversity on a daily basis. Avoidance is usually not the right choice. Embrace your challenges. Analyze your situation. Look at it upside down, inside out, backward, forward, and calmly. Review your options and create a strategy. Above all else, do not be in denial about what is obvious. Remember it is the shark that you do not see that gets you.

ON LIFE

Simple consciousness, which means listening intently and observing, reveals some very interesting information.

LIFE LESSON

When my family was being criminally investigated and eventually charged I learned the power of simple consciousness. I define simple consciousness as being keenly aware of your surroundings and listening intently to what people say and what they don't say. In most cases they will reveal their intentions even if their words are deceptive. Criminal investigators are taught to try and trick suspected persons of interest. Their questions sometimes are indirect but they are trying to manipulate a certain response. Some of us tend to speak more than we listen. Simple consciousness is the opposite. We must listen intently, ask questions, and think about our response. Learn to look at things inside out, upside down, backward, and forward, before coming to a conclusion. I do believe that true simple consciousness can elevate a person's awareness to a level that most humans never experience.

ON LIFE

Happiness is a wise and necessary "CHOICE."

LIFE LESSON

We can choose to be happy and fulfilled individuals. Happiness is not automatic and requires work. Sometimes when we find ourselves in difficult situations with a spouse, a relative, or a friend, always choose happiness. Do not get sucked in by emotional vampires. Your happiness should not be dependent on other people. It is internal and spiritual. Take good care and feed your mind, body, and soul constantly. Make it your personal goal to be a happy, loving, and giving person.

ON LIFE

In life, sometimes too much enthusiasm can become a poison. You will find that the antidote is usually more enthusiasm.

LIFE LESSON

It is impossible to always be happy and uplifting. Enthusiasm, originates from the Greek word "ENTHOUS", meaning, "possessed by a god." Very few endeavors can be accomplished successfully if a person does not have enthusiasm. In the real world there will always be setbacks or challenges that get in the way of your venture. Sometimes people that you care for will be discouraging unintentionally. Do not let anything stop you from accomplishing your goal. Make it your campaign. When discouraged, become enthusiastic or passionate about what you are doing. This year I had the privilege of attending my granddaughter's high school graduation. Ivana Bosch graduated from Rancho Cucamonga High School with a 4.5 point grade average. The entire family was very proud of her. What impressed me very much was the enthusiasm of all of those young people graduating from high school and going out to take on the world. Their hopes and dreams were still in front of them and that positive energy filled the air of the stadium. Yes, they were idealistic and certainly optimistic. I only wish I could bottle that incredible enthusiasm so I could drink it every day.

ON LIFE

True persistence is unconquerable.

LIFE LESSON

Sometimes people give up too quickly. If we want to succeed we must continue to strive to try and reach our goal, in spite of difficulty or opposition. It has been proven that a tiny drop of water that is continuous will break the largest rock over time. Nothing that is valuable comes easy. That includes marriage, raising a family, or education. Even starting a new career can be a daunting challenge. Persist, persist, and persist even more, and you will make yourself unconquerable.

ON LIFE

Discipline yourself for the heart is a treacherous hunter.

LIFE LESSON

We cannot always do what we want or what we feel. It has been said that our desires originate from the heart. We know that the heart does not possess thinking ability, the brain does. Thinking ability is caused by a chemical process within the part of the brain that drives the emotion within the brain. Cognition or the thought process contributes to feelings and our feelings contribute to our behavior.

The figurative heart can betray us, especially in matters of infatuation. The word infatuation comes from the Latin word, "Infature", which literally means, "Make foolish".

ON LIFE

"Pray when you go to bed and sleep but give thanks when you wake." From the book HAVE A LITTLE FAITH.

LIFE LESSON

Most of us are accustomed to praying when we go to bed and go to sleep. When I developed my congestive heart failure, my cardiologist said that my condition causes people to die in their sleep. Now I privately thank God for another day of life when I wake. It might have something to do with getting older and not taking the gift of life for granted. If we had but one day to live, what would we ask God for? We might ask for the opportunity to be with one's spouse and be more loving and kind. We would probably also want to be with our children and tell them how much we love them. There more than likely would be a lot of hugs and kisses. When you wake in the morning each day, God grants this wish to you. Do not take it for granted.

ON LIFE

Love well, love much, love often and show it in your smile.

LIFE LESSON

Love is not just an emotion it also demands action. We start by loving and respecting ourselves. In my opinion, that means being kind to ourselves and taking care of our physical and spiritual needs. Spread your love to your entire family first. Give without expecting anything in return. Love is made to give away and the more you give it away, the more you will receive. The smile comes automatically.

ON LIFE

Taking yourself too seriously spoils all the fun you could be having.

LIFE LESSON

Learn to laugh at yourself. In the larger scheme of things, we really are not that important. My father was a polarizing and dominant figure in my life when I was growing up. I don't remember him ever being happy. It seemed like everything was about him. Now I look back and say, how sad. When he died of cancer in 1981, reality set in. Life goes on and very little changed in his absence. The truth of the matter is, there was more peace, once he passed. He missed out on a lot of fun he could have had with his family and especially his grandchildren. We should not take ourselves so seriously that we forget the fact that none of us are getting out alive. Enjoy your blessings thoroughly every day of your life. Make your life delicious.

ON LIFE

To truly strive to be a decent person is a great pursuit.

LIFE LESSON

I believe that by nature we are imperfect. Good qualities must be developed and maintained. Have you ever heard the saying, "we are creatures of habit?" We all have habits. In most cases they are learned behavior and can become part of our character. It is not always easy to do the right and moral thing. If we strive to be a decent human being, the lasting benefits will be great.

ON LIFE

Make generosity and humility your internal compass.

LIFE LESSON

Being generous is associated with being decent. A truly generous person does not wait to be asked. A truly generous person asks, "How can I help?" Humility is associated with modesty. A humble person can be of great significance but does not have to brag about him or herself. Others will testify as to their greatness. Developing these two qualities, generosity and humility, can guide our path and make us decent human beings.

ON LIFE

"Between stimuli and reaction there is choice." - Dr. Victor Frankel.

LIFE LESSON

We always have choices. Dr. Victor Frankel proved this reality in the most brutal of all Nazi Prison Camps, Auschwitz. Dr. Frankel taught us that choice is present, even if our last choice is to be worthy of our own death. There will always be circumstances that cause us to have to make a choice. That is the stimuli. The choice comes into play when we react to stimuli. Many times when people are confronted with their wrong doings the first thing that comes out of their mouth is, "I don't know, it just happened." In most cases this is self-denial. The truth is that between stimuli, the circumstance or temptation, there is always choice.

ON LIFE

Sometimes being dead wrong is better than being right.

LIFE LESSON

We all have fear and insecurities from time to time. Sometimes we will express our opinions based on those fears and insecurities. This can be a dangerous and slippery slope. It has been my personal experience that when it turns out that I am wrong about a person's intentions or actions, it brings me relief. Being wrong about someone can be a blessing. Embrace it.

ON LIFE

Sometimes you need to, "run silent and run deep."

LIFE LESSON

When I was a boy there was a TV program that dealt with an American submarine and its crew during World War II. When there was a threat from enemy airplanes or destroyers hunting them, the captain would issue the order, "dive, dive, and dive." He would tell his crew, "Run silent, run deep!" In life there are some situations when it is wiser to "run silent, run deep," but always be ready with your periscope.

ON LIFE

Don't sweat the little stuff!

LIFE LESSON

There was a young man, who was asked by his 90-year-old Rabbi, to please say the eulogy at his funeral. It mystified the young man, who had abandoned his faith, that this wise old sage would ask him to say his eulogy. He reluctantly agreed and spent much time in private with the Rabbi who was now near death. This was a great opportunity for the young man to gain great wisdom from this teacher that he admired since his youth. He asked the Rabbi one day, "What is the secret to a long and happy life, Rabbi?" The wise older Rabbi hesitated a little bit while the young man waited for a divine pearl of wisdom. The Rabbi answered, "Don't sweat the little stuff." This was not what the young man expected but truer words have not been spoken.

ON LIFE

It is important sometimes to relearn the things you have been taught.

LIFE LESSON

Our perception can be our reality. It is amazing how much our conviction and points of view can change between 20 and 60 years old. Our life experiences cause us to have to RE-LEARN some things we were taught to us by our parents or teachers. Nothing that is stagnant can live for very long. We should never stop learning. I, for one, will always try to be an idealistic and positive human being. That requires keeping an open mind that is well fed and not afraid of change.

ON LIFE

Everybody has something interesting to say and at least one book to write.

LIFE LESSON

I love people. I love to hear their stories, their life experiences, their hopes and aspirations. Sometimes while talking to older people in their 80s and 90s, that some people might think no longer have purpose, much to my delight, I have discovered and been amazed at the interesting and productive lives some of these people have had. You know the saying, "don't judge a book by its cover," this certainly applies. In future generations, the significance of relatives that came before them is usually lost. Grandchildren and great-grandchildren are left with the task of trying to find out the " TRUTH" about their family tree. We should encourage and even help our parents or grandparents, while they are living, to write about their journeys.

ON LIFE

I refuse to join the religion of victimhood. It requires its followers to worship the false idols of self-pity, anger, and hate.

LIFE LESSON

It has been my experience that some people are dedicated victims. Being a victim has become almost a religion to them. They are constantly feeling sorry for themselves and feel that everybody else gets good opportunities except them. Actually they are very angry people because they feel life has not been fair to them. This is dangerous because that anger can turn into hate. If one always considers themselves victims, their souls will become soiled.

ON LIFE

Sometimes there is not enough time to do things right but always enough time to do it over.

LIFE LESSON

So many times we are in a hurry to complete a project that it seems as if we are running out of time. We convince ourselves that there just is not enough time. It is so much wiser to slow down and take the time needed to complete the project right. That will prevent having to start over again from scratch.

ON LIFE

We become empowered when we realize that in some cases we have no power. Sometimes letting go is really letting God.

LIFE LESSON

When a person is drowning they struggle and thrash their arms desperately trying to stay above water. While struggling they are inhaling water that is going into their lungs. They keep fighting and fighting, sometimes even sink, but manage to fight their way to the surface. Unless help arrives this poor soul drowns and dies. The amazing thing is that when this person is now lifeless and no longer struggling, their body floats to the top. The lesson for us is sometimes hard desperate efforts cause more of a problem than letting go. This is easier said than done; but we must learn our limitations and realize true empowerment and love is a willingness to let go.

ON LIFE

I will share with you a secret that very few people have discovered. It is you, and you alone, who can begin to understand its power. Study and learn about divine inspiration, divine opportunity, and divine intervention. Understanding the way these principles work in our universe will help us obtain clarity and meaning. I cannot provide you a lesson on this matter. You must live it and discover it for yourself!

ON MARRIAGE

Marriage is not a 50-50 proposition it is 100% - 100%. The key to a happy and lasting marriage is both **spouses** dedicating themselves and making the marriage work. They must think married and not think single.

ON MARRIAGE

I find it fascinating, after being married over 44 years, just how intelligent women are. In many cultures, the mother teaches their daughters to be subordinate to men. The sons are exalted in some cases for simply being male. This is why I say, "machismo is a mother's gift to her son and marionismo can be a mother's curse." In order to have a happy and gratifying marriage, spouses should be equal and the respect must be mutual. In a team, every player is equally important, they just play different positions. Married women should never give up their power. Later in life their husbands will thank and praise them.

ON MARRIAGE

Some men might think the grass is greener on the other side. A wife once told her curious husband, "Perhaps your grass would be greener if you watered and attended to it more." Source- Unknown

Jaime Alvarez

ON MARRIAGE

There is a big difference between males and men. Real men create security in their marriages and families. Males, like in the animal kingdom, are controlled by their instincts and hormones not by morality and values.

Eunice and Jaime Married December 2, 1967

ON MARRIAGE

A good way to help ensure a long and happy marriage is to avoid doing the unforgivable.

ON MARRIAGE

I do not believe in a MID-LIFE-CRISIS. It is very possible that this illusion may have been created by men. You seldom hear of a woman's midlife crisis. In most cases, if a woman became promiscuous when reaching midlife, many men would consider her a slut or a cougar. Marriage takes work and devotion. If you choose to be married think and act married.

I remember a meat manager of a Safeway store that I worked at when I was young. His name was Ray. I was only 20 years old and Ray was probably in his early 40s. He was a good-looking Hispanic fellow. Ray was sex crazy except when his wife would show up at the store. He became a totally different man. In front of his wife he would not stare at women's behinds or make vulgar comments under his breath. He had some crazy sayings but the one I remember most was when asked, "Are you married?" His answer was, "No I'm not married but my wife is."

ON MARRIAGE

What is a perfect marriage? A friend once said that she knew a couple who had a perfect marriage because they would never argue. I thought to myself they must never talk to each other. It is impossible, in my opinion, for two intelligent adults to live together and share almost everything to not disagree once in a while. The story of Robinson Caruso comes to mind. When he was stranded on that island, he met a native, and named him Friday. He wanted to teach this man Friday, who was very laid back, his perceived importance of competition. So he marked out a starting line and challenged this good man Friday to a foot race. Friday readily agreed and the race was on. When Robinson Caruso yelled, "GO!," he immediately pulled out ahead and was running as fast as he could, determined to be first in crossing the finish line. Friday, on the other hand, was skipping and whistling during the race. Robinson Caruso waited at the finish line, draped over with his hands on his knees, sweating and breathing hard, as if he was having a heart attack. When Friday finally caught up and finished the race, Robinson Caruso exclaimed, "I won, I won, I beat you." With a big smile, Friday asked, "That is good master. What did you win, may I ask?" The moral of the story is that in marriage, an argument is usually never won, and most of the time the point is not even worth arguing about. Sometimes the next day, when emotions have calmed down, the subject of the argument is not even remembered.

On Parenthood

ON PARENTHOOD

The goal of a good parent is to raise children that will be strong and loving adults that can function without you.

ON PARENTHOOD

The greatest blessing, greatest reward, and life's greatest challenge is to be a good parent. At times it can be very painful but worth it.

ON PARENTHOOD

It has been my personal observation, that it is we the parents, who have the most difficulty in adjusting when the children start growing up. Believe me! I lived it raising four daughters.

ON PARENTHOOD

The most powerful and beneficial lesson that will help your children grow to be decent and productive adults is your good example.

ON PARENTHOOD

Children require loving guidance not brutality. Discipline means to guide not to punish. Praise and compliments have a lasting effect on children.

ON PARENTHOOD

Sometimes being a good parent is not a popularity contest.

ON DAUGHTERS

The greatest blessing and challenge a man can have is raising daughters

ON DAUGHTERS

Your daughter may get married and become another man's wife. There are no guarantees in marriage but a good father is forever. You protect and love your daughters for many years until she becomes a woman. It does not make sense that because she marries you stop being a father.

ON DAUGHTERS

There are very few more rewarding words than to hear your grown daughters say, "It is like dad always said." It brings a special hidden smile to a father's heart.

Left to Right,
Gina Bosch, Marisela Labastida, Eunice Alvarez,
Leticia Eastland, Jaime Alvarez, Elena Labastida

On Grandchildren

Grandchildren signal a new beginning of the rest of your life. Embrace it! When grandchildren come into our lives, we are usually at a different stage than when we were raising our own children. It is so much easier to admire all the cute and silly things they do. They are little people that warm our hearts. Some people say that grandparents spoil their grandchildren, to that I say, ABSOLUTELY! That's what being a grandparent is all about. Grandchildren are truly the seeds that matter.

Left to Right,
Jenaru Eastland, Sophia Bosch, Hector Labastida, Victor Labastida, Ivana Bosch, Vivian Bosch, Jasmine Eastland, Priscila Merriman, Isaac Labastida, Katrina Labastida, Eunice Alvarez, Leonardo Labastida, Jaime Alvarez, John Jaime Eastland, Seth Labastida

On Friends

ON FRIENDS

True friendship starts with yourself. You cannot be a good friend if you neglect your mind, body, and soul. A burden is what you will become and not a supportive ally.

ON FRIENDS

Give your friends more than you expect from them.

ON FRIENDS

We do not get to choose who our relatives are but we certainly can choose who are friends will be.

ON FRIENDS

Learn to know the difference between a true friend and an acquaintance.

ON FRIENDS

Make your friends before you need them. Never take advantage of this sacred bond.

THE SEEDS ARE WHAT MATTER!

Left to Right,
Sophia Bosch, Leonardo Labastida, Isaac Labastida, Vivian Bosch

Left to Right,
Sophia Bosch, Jaime Alvarez, Isaac Labastida,
Vivian Bosch, Leonardo Labastida

Katrina Labastida

$$\mathcal{O}n\,Gardening$$

ON GARDENING

My garden taught me that it is the seeds that matter. Everything starts out as a seed, even us!

ON GARDENING

The cycle of life is ever present in the garden. For example, my tomato plants that I plant every year so my wife can make salsa. Sometimes I get volunteer tomatoes. These are tomatoes that came back on their own from seeds. Every tomato that is produced by their plant has seeds. Eventually the tomato plant gets old and dies. The seeds are more important as they continue to produce more tomato plants. It reminds me of our grown children. Eunice and I have four married daughters. They are all married and have children of their own. Soon I will be 63 years old and I've been married for 44 years. I am like the tomato plant that is beginning to wither. My fruit are my daughters and they are in the prime of their life. Their seeds, which are our grandchildren, are our replacements. It is important that we nurture and take good care of the new seeds for they are what matter.

ON GARDENING

Gardening is more spiritual than physical. Gardening is hard work. You must prepare the ground ahead of time, probably in the fall or winter. This is all done before you even begin to plant. Weeds will have to be removed and dirt tilled more than once, then comes the mulch and fertilizer your garden requires. Weeds of all kind will be your constant enemy. With all that said, it is amazing to see the birth of newborn plants being born from the ground and beginning to reach for the sun. There is a great sense of pride for the gardener as the plant grows to be healthy and strong. When the first flowers begin to blossom you know that your hard work will produce delicious and healthy vegetables. It is truly amazing to witness the growing plants become pregnant and produce their offspring. Even though the gardener tills the land, it is God who makes it grow. For those who garden it is a spiritual experience.

ON GARDENING

The greatest compliment you can bestow on a flower is to choose it for a beautiful bouquet that everyone will admire.

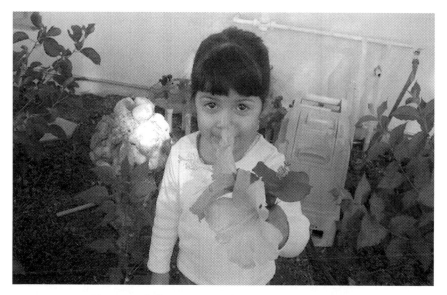

Photos Include Vivian Bosch and Katrina Labastida

ON GARDENING

Gardeners have a special relationship with their plants. The flowers in a rose garden come in all shapes and colors. Some are fragrant and long stemmed while some are not. My plants produce so many beautiful roses that it is hard to choose the flower that will grace a bouquet. There are very special flowers that are so beautiful that they earn the right to be part of a special bouquet. When they are chosen and placed in a vase, they are so beautiful that everybody that enters the room will stop and admire enjoying their fragrance. The majority of people will only worship them when they are displayed as part of a magnificent bouquet.

ON GARDENING

Gardening is a lot like life, the harder you work, the more successful your garden will be.

ON GARDENING

Some people will say that a gardener has a green thumb. Usually it is people that do not garden very much that will make such a comment. Gardening is hard work, but most things in life that are of value require hard work. It is like the saying, "The harder I work, the luckier I get." The beauty of getting young children involved in gardening is that they will learn the value and benefit of work. It will also teach them generosity, when they give away as gifts the fruits and vegetables that they had a part in growing. Remember, you cannot have a garden without a gardener.

ON GARDENING

Volunteers are sometimes the most resilient of plants. Volunteers are plants that are born from seeds you did not plant. For example, when tomatoes fall to the ground, some of the seeds become embedded in the soil. Sometimes birds will eat the seeds and replant them, fertilizing them along the way. It has been my experience that volunteer plants are some of the heartiest and most productive plants in my garden.

ON GARDENING

If you are willing to see and listen to plants in your garden, they will talk to you and even dance for you. When a gardener is truly involved with his or her plants there is a certain communication that occurs between them. The plant will let you know when they need water because they will get sad and wilt. A good gardener will worry about the plants almost like if they were related to each other. Of course, the plant is very dependent on the diligence of their friend, the gardener. Plants will show their gratitude by springing up and thanking the gardener for watering it. On a windy day, they will sway back and forth to the music of the wind, as if they were dancing for you.

ON GARDENING

One of the greatest benefits of gardening is that you can truly see the good of your hard work. We all want to be rewarded for our hard work. Gardening provides and satisfies this need. Personally I enjoy a delicious beer or glass of wine while I admire the beauty of my garden in the evening. There is a sense of accomplishment when you enjoy the food from your garden.

ON GARDENING

Garden plants demonstrate God's generosity. The more you pick their fruit, the more the plant gives. I love to give tomatoes, squash, onions and chili peppers to as many people as possible. This is a great life lesson. The more we give, the more we will receive.

ON GARDENING

Gardening is a lot like raising children. The most challenging and rewarding experience in my life has been raising my four daughters. I can only speak from my personal experience in this matter. When they were born, they were brought home to a very loving environment, prepared by their great mother. Like seedlings, babies and children require special care. Their mother, Eunice, watched over and nursed them like a mother lioness watches over her cubs. Our babies were never neglected. As they began to grow, just like the plants in the garden, other challenges became manifest. This was especially true in their teen age years. In the garden, you are always battling weeds which are very resilient and determined. These dominant weeds can corrupt or harm your plants. Sometimes you can't identify weeds until it is too late. When raising children there is a biblical principle that should always be remembered by parents, "Bad associations spoil good habits." Some kids that come into your children's lives are exactly like weeds. They are determined to corrupt your plants and seeds. The garden requires constant vigilance and attention.

ON GARDENING

The other day I was looking for a jalapeno chili pepper in my garden for my wife's salsa. As I looked at the front of the chili plant I could not find any ripe chilies. With my hand on my chin I stared intently at the chili plant. As much as I tried, I couldn't see the right size chilies! I went around the plant to look at the other side from a different angle. Much to my surprise, there were at least a dozen perfect jalapenos that I could see from this different angle. It is very easy to get tunnel vision. Sometimes when we insist on looking at a matter in just one way, we don't benefit from seeing the possibilities. Just like in the garden, I have learned to look at things upside down, inside out, backward and forward. A different perspective can be a very positive experience.

ON GARDENING

You can identify a plant by its fruit. The same is true about people.

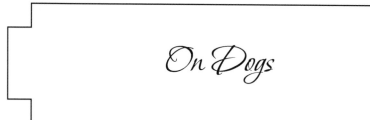

ON DOGS

My dogs name is "Shamu." He is a funny looking little dog whose hair covers his eyes and he has a serious under-bite. I didn't want him but he wanted me. Now we are both happy. You don't own a dog, they own you.

ON DOGS

We can learn a lot from dogs. They can teach humans about the power of persistence. Their loyalty is something we as humans should emulate.

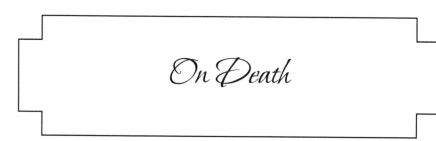

On Death

ON DEATH

A parent's worst fear is to have one of their children die before they do.

COMMENT

Nothing that I can imagine can be as devastating as to lose one of your children. In my mind, the natural order of things is that our children bury us. Let us not take one single day for granted and love our children with our hearts and souls. Even in this crazy busy life we live, we must take time out and spend it with our children. We should never take them for granted.

ON DEATH

Death is our least desired inevitability.

COMMENT

Death is an unbreakable contract with life itself. It must be eventually honored. Time and circumstance may allow for a deferment but the debt is always collected. Understanding this reality teaches us to live each day as if it was our last.

ON DEATH

Death is not the worst thing that can happen to us, capitulating our values is!

COMMENT

We all eventually die. Dr. Victor Frankel during his terrible ordeal in the Nazi concentration camp Auschwitz said that all he had remaining and could control was to be "worthy of his death." Dr. Frankel refused to capitulate his values in order to save his skin. The Nazis were never able to break his resolve. We should not have a morbid fear of death in the physical sense. Worse than death is a broken spirit that merely exists.

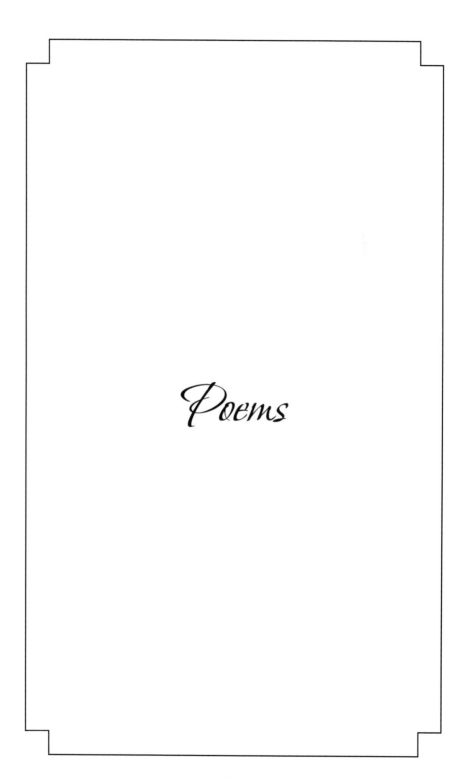

Poems

Jaime Alvarez

Over the years I have written many poems. Sad to say the majority have been lost or misplaced. What I have provided is a sample of some of my more recent poems. I try to frame the context of the situation that inspired me to write the poem.

One day while looking at a beautiful picture of my four daughters when they were little girls, I was inspired to write this poem. We had taken our four little girls to Disneyland and they were riding the boat in the IT'S A SMALL WORLD ride. They looked so happy and secure. You can see how they were taking care of their little sister, Gina, and showing her the different scenes. What I love most is how close they were. Even today their love and closeness for each other is stronger than ever.

Dreams Captured In Time

This special picture captures our hopes and dreams.

A father's wishes are framed forever.

You cannot see my smile, but it's there, and with pride I did beam.

It's a lifetime that is important, not a fleeting moment, and yet it is that moment this picture captures and freezes.

As a father, I can only see happiness in my daughters smiles, beautifully captured for the rest of time.

Life is hard because of its many changes, many of which are born of pain.

Today it seems that I have traded places with my beloved daughters. The baton has been passed along with its gain.

The gains are a father's best efforts to be strong and who tried to do what seemed right.

In life, the natural order of things cannot be stopped. It is as constant as the day following night.

I have become a shadow of the man I once was. This is neither progressive nor degenerative but normal.

To say that life is but a fleeting moment is one thing, but to actually experience it, is the greatest lesson of all.

There is very little control, very little strength, and certainly no power.

A very temporary presentation, just like a new season that is born, but disappears as quickly as the presence of its wildflower.

The smiles captured in this picture beam of confidence and hope.

The dreams they whispered have not been silenced but are different now. Time and circumstance have made it so and for this we must allow.

For a mother and father this picture fulfills their role. The little daughter's in the picture now have the stage.

Their children have now grown with the speed of a dream. The eternal book of life has turned that page.

Eunice's Poem

December 2, 2011

44 years ago, on December 2, 1967, we became one.

At 62 years old, I can look back with gratitude because it was the best thing I have ever done.

We were 14 years young when we met.

How ironic that it was at a funeral on a rainy day which I will never forget.

At 18 years old, we married, not really knowing where we were going nor what we had begun.

It didn't matter that we had no plan. We just looked into each other's eyes and you held my hand.

Throughout these many years we have never looked back with regret. When we look back at our journey together, it's to celebrate.

Our marriage was the beginning of our amazing run.

What has kept us together these 44 years is our love, our common purpose, and a willingness to learn.

Together we raised our four daughters and every day their love we tried to earn.

Mom was like a lioness that protected and nurtured our cubs and I was the male lion working hard to bring food for our pride.

The challenges have been many, some unthinkable and dark, but our love and strength did not permit us to run and hide.

Sometimes in our private and quiet moments, we talk about our past mostly with a smile, but sometimes we cannot help but to shake our heads in disbelief.

Throughout it all, except once, we knew our God would be our salvation and bring relief.

Now in 2011, we have been married 16,060 days.

These are the days of our lives and we have experienced winter, spring, summer, and fall in our journey along the way.

Through it all our family was our purpose. This mutual understanding, born of love, made us strong together.

Thank you for being my wife. I would ask for 44 more years, but instead, I will ask you to be with me forever.

Your Husband

Leticia's Poem

My eldest daughter is Leticia. On October 27, 2011, she turned 43 years old. Your firstborn child always maintains a special place in your life. The first child marks a new beginning of the rest your life.

TO MY FIRST BORN

Today you turned 43 years old and it is your special day.

It is very significant because you are our first born child; it is your special place even today.

When you came into our lives you were truly a blessing. You introduced mom and I to a new life and helped us learn so many wonderful things.

To cuddle and love your own baby for the first time is divine. The experience is covered with joy but also the fear only a firstborn brings.

I will always remember when you first began to crawl in our second story apartment you discovered our locked screen front door.

That became your first view of the world. You would race on your hands and knees to this special place excited with baby courage ready to explore.

Sometimes a loud truck would roar down the street, you would turn wide-eyed and crawl back on your hands and knees to mom and I.

After feeling safe in your mother's arms for just a little while, you would muster up the courage and return back to your screen door to stare at the beautiful blue sky.

Today, mom and I, look into that same sky with grateful eyes. We remember all the happiness you have brought into our lives.

Now you're the CHARGE NURSE of your little world, with a husband and grown children. Your mom and I still have the memories of our first born child which we will always remember with a smile and a sigh.

Love Dad

Marisela's Poem

This next poem I wrote for my daughter MARISELA on her 42nd birthday. I make a habit of writing poems on all special occasions.

HAPPY SPECIAL DAY, October 6, 2011

On October 6, 1969, I was working at the West Covina Safeway Store when I heard the telephone ring.

"I know you don't like me calling my husband while he is working but I am ready to have this baby so tell him to get home now, "my wife Eunice screamed.

Out the door I ran with my meat cutter apron still on. I drove as fast as I could and with all my strength to the steering wheel I did cling.

Slow-moving trucks, red signal lights, and stop signs, were blocking my arrival as if it was on purpose, so it seemed.

When I finally made it home, my young wife was waiting with tears in her eyes. She had a very worried look on her face and I knew she was scared.

You were not ready to be born and complications had accompanied the pregnancy. The doctors had warned us of the dangerous possibilities so we could be prepared.

Once again you fooled them all. You were born healthy weighing over eight pounds. Yes, you were perfect, much to our delight.

Seems like yesterday, a 19-year-old father and mother, brought home their baby girl with hearts full of gratitude and love.

You were very special then, as you are today. As your father it's still hard for me to comprehend that you are 42.

Now you have raised children of your own. You have been blessed with family. That makes you very proud because you have learned that it is our children that teach us the real meaning of life.

Some people are Islands, living their lives empty of love, but not you. Your life is rich because you strive to be a great person, mother, and wife.

Your household will always be full of laughter and joy. It is God's gift to you and your husband. Your children you embrace every day.

So, I sneak you a happy birthday as a celebration of life. No cake, no candles, no singing happy birthday because that is our way.

Love Dad

Elena's Poem

My third daughter is Elena Labastida. She was born February 1, 1972. She married her husband, Victor when she was sixteen years old. They celebrated their 24th wedding anniversary, February 2012. Her birthday and her wedding anniversary are almost on the same day.

HAPPY 24TH WEDDING ANNIVERSARY ELENA AND VIC

I almost went into atrial fibrillation when your mother told me you would be forty years old.

The bullet train of life that we all ride carries a precious cargo that is worth more than gold.

Our lives are its valuable cargo for us to enjoy but the bullet train travels much too fast.

Embrace every day of your life. Love everything God has blessed you with and make every minute last.

When you were little I taught you and your sisters the secret of the TIME MACHINE.

If you imagined hard enough, then projected your thoughts into the future when you had a problem, you could leave that scene.

It worked so well that now we wish it could slow down and be brought to a halt.

Now I wish I could dismantle the TIME MACHINE that works too well. I would take it and hide it in a secret vault.

As much as I would want to do this, or even try, time is unforgiving it forces us to be realistic.

Our nature is complex and our journey is full of hills and valleys, sometimes even danger. When you were little it seemed more comfortable and simplistic.

A mother and father always remember their babies, even when they are in their 40's. You are our child celebrating the 24th anniversary of your wedding day.

You were always much older than your years.

Today, you and Vic, have much to reflect on. Together you have traveled so far. With loving experience, it is words of wisdom you will say.

In this World being married twenty four years is a great accomplishment.

When you and Vic see your two great sons, family, and friends, you can both say, thank you Almighty God, for all these blessings YOU sent.

Love Dad

Gina's Poem

My baby daughter is Gina Bosch. On her 36th birthday, I wrote her this poem.

HAPPY SPECIAL DAY GINA

On October 7, 1975, in Brawley California, the most beautiful baby in the World was born.

Even the doctors and nurses in the delivery room proclaimed her so.

When you were a baby I would hold your little hands and you would jump as high as you could to make me smile.

I was a proud young Father then. If only I had known that these precious moments would only last a little while.

Today is October 7, 2011 and you are 36 years old on this day.

When you were born I knew that you were special and would be strong, beautiful and kind as you made your way.

Into marriage and motherhood you have ventured with your mind, body, and soul.

You give all your love to your three beautiful daughters and no greater love will the World behold.

Some people do not celebrate birthdays and that is fine for them. But to me it is a celebration of life.

Tonight, I will raise my glass of wine to the heavens and thank our Creator for my baby daughter who has become a great mother and wife.

Love Dad

A Tsunami Called Life

This poem I wrote on my 58th birthday. It was a very difficult time for our entire family. All my daughters and my wife were being persecuted by what I came to call the criminal *injustice* system. I felt very sad and hurt that I could not protect my family the way I was used to. When one sees the force of a Tsunami you realize the unstoppable force of nature. It destroys everything made by man in its path. At this point in time, I felt that my life had been caught up in a Tsunami. That is why I entitled this poem, "A TSUNAMI CALLED LIFE."

A TSUNAMI CALLED LIFE

On the day of my fifty eighth birthday I have much to be thankful about.

The challenges of life have not been able to break my spirit because I have learned that there is always an in and there will be an out.

Let me share this understanding with you, my loved ones, this moment, this day.

Life is not about taking and it is not about hoarding. It is about the ability to do good, for this we must pray.

The greatest sins are sins of omission when we could have made a difference but were too tired or scared to try.

This is what life is all about, never giving up, striving every day and every minute, about this I cannot lie.

At fifty eight, I have seen the ones broken and battered by this Tsunami called life.

Or was it that they were their own worst enemy and they alone created their disaster and strife?

The Tsunami called life has really never changed. It has been like a force of nature whose power we must respect and try to understand.

To unleash life's destructive force with reckless and selfish acts is like purposely planting poisonous weeds on good land.

It should not surprise us than that we are weakened and made sick by indulging without restraint on this poisonous food.

At first it made us feel happy and free but it was the life of a fool that seemed so carefree and good.

We cannot blame the Tsunami called life for our selfish choices that we planned and created for the fleshly pleasure of our own.

I cannot lie against the truth because this is what I have seen much too close for me to be remiss.

But I have also seen the beauty and joy of life for which there is not a painful price to pay.

The fruits of good land that was worked and watered, of which I had a part in growing.

Not just one generation but three, and maybe four, if it is God's will.

To this I am committed and I will fight our enemies with cunning wisdom and skill.

It takes great courage to live this life but it also takes love, patience and perseverance in order to reap the fullness of the crop.

So many times I wished I could make it easier for my loved ones when I would see their struggle with their own strife.

I look back and remember my own life with my four daughters and a very young wife.

It was those times of battle and struggle filled with fear and uncertainty that made us appreciate deliverance by Almighty God at his right time.

We would not be who we are today if we had not gone through that pain. I will never forget the moments that seemed impossible and I thought my God was gone.

Looking back I see now it was God, and God alone that sustained us. He was constant and loving but it was I who stubbornly did not want to move on.

When this Tsunami called life seems to overwhelm you and you are sure that you are about to drown.

It's probably time for change, time for a new beginning, time to look to the heavens to God, but never look down.

Written by Jaime Alvarez

My Friend the Wind

MY FRIEND THE WIND, I wrote one day when I was remembering how close I came to dying in 2007. I wrote it for my daughters in an effort to help them feel secure about my resolve to fight and continue living. That day, I was in my garden, the wind was blowing and that was my inspiration.

MY FRIEND THE WIND

Indulge me my daughters, on this day that I turn sixty years old.

Once my friend the wind came to sweep me away and I said, "I can't go, please let me stay".

My friend the wind said, "I come from the heavens, the mountains and the sea, you cannot tell me when to take you away."

My friend the wind continued, "I come from the north, south, west and east, I do not ask you what to do or say!"

"The leaves I move throughout the earth are mine, your request to stay is uncommon, but not out of line".

"I know your works. Many times I have swept over them with great care, that gentle breeze you felt meant that I was there.

Yes, I am your friend but remember only I can make the trees howl or bring forth a hurricane so be cautious about what you ask and from insistence you must refrain.

So tell me, why should I not remove you from this Earth this very moment, may I ask?"

I humbly responded, "Please my friend, all these things I know you can do, but there exists a task. For your kindness I will serve your MASTER, who allows you to Exist. I have no strength or power of my own and it is in His name that I insist."

You see, my friend, I have made a promise to help others and this I must keep.

So please for this reason allow me to awaken from my sleep."

JAIME ALVAREZ, September 14, 2009

Things I learned at Sixty

Every birthday I like to take some time to reflect on my life and all the blessings that God has given me. In this poem I try to communicate some of my personal experiences and opinions on life.

WHAT I HAVE LEARNED AT SIXTY

Today I am sixty years old. It's a good time to look back and remember.

What comes to mind is my mother. In 1949, she was only twenty three years old, that fateful September.

At sixty years old, I have learned the relativity of time and space.

On September 14, 1949, I was only a few hours old and certainly in another place.

Hours became days and days became years, sixty to be exact.

The passing of time has not been in vain. To be a decent human being with God I made a pact.

That does not mean I am perfect. I embrace the reality that I will not be around forever.

I have much work to do, starting with myself. To be kinder, more loving, and wiser I will endeavor.

At sixty years old I appreciate the people in my life that I call friends. To me they have become more valuable than gold.

I want to be a tender person loyal and true this is more important to me as I get old.

But old is a relative term, for a single day can be a lifetime depending on your circumstance.

Sixty years old is a relatively long time but in the massive river of time it is but a glance.

It is knowing that we are very temporary that makes us treasure every moment of the day.

I have learned to embrace life's ups and downs. Whether they are good or bad, loyal to my conscience I will stay.

September 14, 2009

Things I learned at Sixty-One

THINGS I HAVE LEARNED AT SIXTY-ONE YEARS OLD, is a list of reflections and thoughts that I have accumulated throughout my lifetime. It was September 14, 2011, and I was in a very reflective mood so I wrote down some of the thoughts and conclusions that I have come to personally.

THINGS I HAVE LEARNED AT SIXTY-ONE YEARS OLD

GOD

Our God is a benevolent God and not a punitive one. He loves me much more than I could ever love him. At times I have betrayed him, but he has never betrayed me.

ATTITUDE

Trees die at the top. We all age and that is inevitable, but our attitude toward the meaning of our lives does not die at the top, but certainly can live at the top.

TIME

Where did time go? We might ask. Time stays. It is we that go and much too quickly. So let's live our lives to the fullest every day.

ISLANDS

I have witnessed the sad tragedy of those who choose to become islands. They are never happy nor fulfilled. Even in the middle of a village they are still alone.

VICTIMS

I refuse to belong to the religion of victimhood. It requires its followers to worship the false idols of self-pity, anger and hate.

INITIATIVE

There are those who step back in order to avoid being involved. Then there are those who step forward frequently and never ask "why didn't anybody tell me?" or "why am I always the go last to know?"

MOUNTAINS

Don't make mountains out of mole hills. Life is too short to sweat the small stuff. It is also too precious to waste our time on negative thoughts or negative people.

FRIENDS

Friends are precious and few. They should be cherished and never forsaken. You cannot choose who your relatives are but you can choose your friends.

MATERIALISM

It is not money that is the root of all evil, but rather, the love of money. Love is reserved for special people in our lives. This is part of our sacred service to our Creator. The hoarding of material possessions is neither wise nor fulfilling. In most cases, material possessions emphasize what you have, and not who you really are. Materialism creates a self-imposed loneliness.

LIFE AND DEATH

You cannot really live if you do not have something you are willing to die for. The worst death is a slow and miserable existence controlled by fear and guilt. To live is to risk and not be readily satisfied with the status quo. Living is about giving our best effort and it should always start at home.

RELATIVITY OF TIME

When I was a young man of 21 years old, I worked at a Meat Plant, owned by the Ralph's Grocery Company. I had moved from the Safeway Plant that had over 2,000 employees. Ralph's was much smaller with only 400 employees. I was young and full of beans with endless energy. One day I was working next to one of the old-timers, Don Oldham. It was only 15 minutes before going home time. I looked at my watch and told Don, "15 minutes left, that's nothing!" Don responded in his calm elderly voice, "that depends, if you are hanging or praying, 15 minutes is a long time."

Jaime Alvarez

A Bullet Train Called Life

I am sixty two years old and I ask myself, where did time go?

Yesterday, I was a child and the next day a young man, with a wife and children. That was almost fifty years ago.

Today I am a grandfather of many, thirteen to be exact.

I ride the bullet train of life and eternal time is its conductor, not I, that's a fact.

As I age it seems that the bullet train of life is reaching a greater speed.

My destination is clear, and I accept the inevitable, which will come much too soon for me. It's final call I shall heed.

I do not fear getting old, but I want to live every day to its fullest, leaving nothing incomplete.

Loving and hugging all my loved ones every day, embracing life's reinvention of me and never allowing for defeat.

I think I have learned how to slow down this train I ride, even though when I look at myself in the mirror, a different story is told.

My goal is to grab and hold every minute and every hour of each day that I live. It has been said, "Trees die at the top." My body will age but my mind will always be young and bold.

Jaime Alvarez

Laughter

I have been accused of always smiling, to me that is a good thing. Laughter and smiling are exclusive to human beings. It is amazing how powerful laughter is.

LAUGHTER

August 6, 2010

It is only humans that have been given this gift.

Laughter is contagious and our sagging spirits it will lift.

Sometimes it is subtle and other times it can be a roar.

It starts in our heart and burst from our mouth leaving us wanting much more.

To laugh together with loved ones and friends is the greatest laughter of all.

When you laugh so hard that tears of joy begin to flow, our differences like weakened walls will fall.

Of course the most important and purest laughter is directed at ourselves, never the misfortune of others.

Jaime Alvarez

To be able to laugh at ourself requires the dismissing of our foolish pride.

Laughing will make us much happier souls. Learn to laugh at unforgiving changes that come with aging. This laughter can only be shared with your bride.

Jaime Alvarez

Reflections on Dying

In 2007 I came very close to dying due to congestive heart failure and atrial fibrillation. To complicate matters, a large blood clot had developed in the back of my heart. One Cardiologist secretly told my wife and daughters, that they should take me home and let me spend my last days there. My heart had been beating at almost 200 beats per minute probably for months. This was a very sobering and serious predicament. The nine days I spent in intensive care at the hospital gave me a great opportunity to reflect on my life and the real possibility of dying.

DYING

I am not afraid of dying because I know my life has had meaning.

I will be remembered fondly, not by all men, but certainly by those whom I loved.

My legacy will be one of strength, courage, and honesty, but above all else decency.

My greatest dragons that I have had to conquer are anger and fear.

They were inside my heart and mind but did not infect my soul.

Every day I will thank God for giving me back my soul when I wake.

Jaime Alvarez

Just like my loved ones, every day is special and a gift.

Since I am not afraid of dying, I will never fear living and loving with all my spirit.

Jaime Alvarez

Love

I inherited many wonderful qualities from my beloved mother. She was not a person that would drown you with kisses and hugs, but it is because of her that I became the man I am today.

MY KIND OF LOVE

I have sometimes been accused of not being tender and loving enough.

To a certain degree it must be true because it is those who love me the most that have made this comment.

The love and value of those who I would die for is enough to make me stop and reflect.

I think I created a shell that I thought was necessary. Tenderness and feeling I did neglect.

My guilt and fault in this regard is mine to own but perhaps in my perceived need to be strong and a warrior I was wrong.

There is no attempt to make an excuse or justify but my heart tells me that it's time for me to sing a new song.

Many times I have asked myself, "Why me?" "Why did I have to be the one who jumped forward to protect?"

As a child amongst the screams and tears, I saw everybody petrified with fear. That violence required me to answer with my violence, this I did not request.

The insanity of my youth's violent circumstances drowned my senses and I refused to feel pain.

Pain would only dull my senses. Then I would not be alert, ready to confront the man that was supposed to be our father and should protect.

I buried my pain, but it showed in my face. I absorbed a million hurts and disappointments, I unwillingly became their collector.

I admit that tenderness and outward display of affection is not part of my profile, this I understand.

My life has changed for the better so much. My perceived necessities have also been replaced. Please remember how far I have come when you see me lovingly kissing and holding my grandchildren's hand.

Written by a husband, father, and grandfather.

The Way We Are

One of my favorite songs is, "The way we were," by Barbara Streisand. That is why this poem is entitled, "THE WAY WE ARE." I wrote this poem when my entire family was going through the most difficult time in our history. We had been criminally charged by the County of San Bernardino District Attorney and we knew the charges were totally false. When you are in a crisis of this magnitude, it is important to reflect on your blessings.

THE WAY WE ARE

A beautiful song once asked, "If we had to it all again could we, would we?"

"Was it all so simple then or has time rewritten every line?"

For me it was all so simple then! As I look back in time at sixty two.

My wife raised our four beautiful daughters and created a beautiful environment for them to grow while I worked away from home.

I was always secure in knowing our little castle was safe and my children were always clean and well fed.

As for me getting to our home and being all together was my only goal.

Yes it was "OH SO SIMPLE THEN" and yes, "TIME HAS REWRITTEN EVERY LINE."

Our blessings continue to grow because of all our new seeds.

As hard as these times were, we are still blessed, and these are our best times.

We have health and above all else we have unity and love. If we measure our strengths we can appreciate these continued blessings.

So we must choose to remember and immerse ourselves in all that is good and great in our lives.

The amazing truth is, the way we are is the reason we took the stance we did. Our love for each other is why we are so blessed.

That is why we can all say with great pride and gratitude, this is truly, "THE WAY WE ARE."

Jaime Alvarez

Fallen Skies

FALLEN SKIES

The skies are blue and bright. My skies are dark and grey.

The storms of war are in my sight, not sun, not day, not light.

Only thunder and lightning fill the sky.

A doomsday storm, that has to come, started by men that lie.

They have pierced my heart and at times leave me numb.

God forgive and help me with the hate I have.

Give me strength to live without this curse, and be happy, till the day I die.

Jaime Alvarez

Our Village Came Together

Our family is our village. This poem I wrote during a tragic period that caused much pain. As imperfect humans we all make mistakes. The village will never abandon one of its own.

OUR VILLAGE CAME TOGETHER

Our Village is strong, but caring and always growing.

We try to be examples of true love, like a lantern in the dark that is glowing.

No, we are not perfect, that makes us try harder.

We strive to love and protect one another and all become wiser and smarter.

To the Village, the seeds are what matter, the planter knows this fact.

In Godly devotion, we walk living by the way we act.

There are times the Village must rally around one who fell.

That's the power of the Village, with love it creates a protective shell.

Injury comes in many forms; it could be illness, fatigue or a serious mistake.

By the Grace of God, the Village will help our loved one heel, and do whatever it takes.

Like a golden pond that has been hit with a large rock, it sinks to the bottom without causing harm.

The people of our Village are like the calming ripples that create small waves that absorb the blow, only to return to its calm, after the alarm.

A stranger could look upon that pond and say "If my life could only be so calm".

Not knowing the challenges experienced by the Village, the need for prayers and wisdom of the Psalms.

The Village will survive and be strong, because in Gods spirit it will place trust.

Not in man's worldly treasures that accumulate rust.

We must always remember, it is a privilege to be part of our Village. We all should help to make it secure. When any of us needs help, the Village will come together for you, of that you can be sure.

Grandfather

November 18, 2006

The day we went to retrieve one of our OWN.

Precious Stones

In May of 2008 when I almost died I made a promise to myself. If God gave me life, I would always try to lift the spirits of those who are downtrodden. In my own way I have been true to my commitment. PRECIOUS STONES is a poem that I was inspired to write for two very dear friends that were going through a terrible and unjust criminal investigation. It was my way of trying to lift their spirits.

PRECIOUS STONES

In our short and quick lifetime, we learn to appreciate the special people God has placed in our space.

Space is that dimension of time through which we all race.

At times the journey can become hectic, but it is mostly a wonderful opportunity to be shared with others in dignity and grace.

When I think of your loving kindness, I realize that our friendship was born of trust. A special bond was formed that time cannot erase.

I know there have been unsolicited and unjust moments filled with uncertainty and fear.

Through it all we must believe that we are protected and know that your friends are always near.

Jaime Alvarez

Both of you are very special people that God has united in spirit and love.

Two soul mates intertwined forever and given a special mission directed from above.

This world finds it impossible to understand goodness and the sincerity of special people like you.

If they had spiritual eyes the simplicity of greatness would be revealed, but this gift is only for a few.

We cannot expect those whose eyes and souls are soiled with suspicion and doubt, to understand or relate.

Why should they be so privileged when what they embrace is strife and hate?

Your true friends know the beautiful people, both of you are.

Every day we give thanks and pray that you will be safe and from our thoughts you are never far.

Please continue to be strong for us and let your benevolence reign.

Your blessings and accomplishments are many times greater than those few moments of passing pain.

It is we who need both of you to be strong so that goodness and loyalty can win.

No matter what evil may try, God has placed rings around you and they will protect you from harm and men's sin.

The secret to your victory will be your faith, love for God, and each other.

You are both precious stones, yes diamonds, and we all know diamonds last forever

Your friend, Jaime

Thinking of You

This poem was written to the same friends that I wrote Precious Stones for. One morning, as I always do, I woke up early made our coffee and went out to work in my garden. Out of nowhere the thought of my two friends came to me, so I wrote "THINKING OF YOU."

THINKING OF YOU

I woke up this morning very early and while drinking my coffee in my garden, I was thinking of you.

It is the first day of spring, and even though it is a little cold, a new season begs to be born in spite of the morning dew.

I could feel the change that nature was bringing so could my flowers and trees. Even the sparrows were singing a new tune.

Maybe my spirit was moved because a new season and new adventure in both of your blessed lives will be starting soon.

Change of this magnitude is always filled with mixed emotions of gratitude and a little sorrow.

You have done so much for all of us. Our lives have been enriched by your unwavering friendship. Now it's time to start your beautiful tomorrow.

Time is God's greatest gift. You have wisely chosen to share your gift with friends, but more importantly, your beloved family.

Family is our true treasure on this Earth. They are the seeds that matter. History and experience will always prove this blessed reality.

Please keep close to your heart the collective love and gratitude of all your friends. We will always admire your dignity and grace.

Soon there will be new candidates and a fresh campaign for your seat. The truth is nobody can ever take your place.

Your friend, JAIME

True Life Stories

Experiences At The Safeway Meat Plant In Vernon, California

1970

In 1967, I wanted to get married with my childhood sweetheart, Eunice. The only problem was that I was only 17 years old and a senior in high school without a job. My father had worked in the grocery business on and off. He suggested trying to become an apprentice meat cutter. He drove me to Safeway's regional offices on Melrose Avenue in Hollywood. This is where Safeway would give me an aptitude test and interview. After the interview I was told that my score was very good, but at 17 years old, the company's insurance policy would not cover me as an apprentice meat-cutter. They proposed I become a box boy for about six months until I turned 18. They placed me at the Safeway store in El Monte. My job would be bagging food for customers and bringing in shopping carts.

My ultimate goal was to become an apprentice meat-cutter when I turned 18 years old. I considered it a privilege and great opportunity to have this job. My baseball training as captain of the varsity baseball team served me well. I would run to bring in the empty shopping carts that were in the parking lot as if I was stealing second base. Management loved my hustle but the other box boys with more seniority didn't appreciate it. In fact, the senior box boy told me to slow down because I was making them look bad. He was telling an All-

Star third baseman to make a few errors deliberately and become mediocre. It was not going to happen. Finally on September 14, 1967, I turned 18. I will never forget when the district manager and the regional meat supervisor came to the store to interview me. The regional meat supervisor was a good-looking man in his early 40s. He asked me what I planned to do and why did I want to be a meat cutter? I told him, in front of the district manager, that I intended to get married in December and that I wanted to have a good trade and career with Safeway. The meat supervisor asked in disbelief, "Why do you want to do that? You're only 18 years old?" Before I could answer, the district manager, who was his superior, stated "That's good. We want you to be tied down. Being married with a family helps secure Safeway's investment in you." I told the district manager, "Thank you sir." In front of his boss and very unwillingly the meat supervisor said, "Congratulations on your upcoming wedding."

My meat cutter apprenticeship started in September of 1967. I became a journeyman meat-cutter in 1969. Once I became a journeyman I was required to work nights and weekends. With a wife and two baby daughters there wasn't much choice in the matter. My goal was to become the best and fastest meat cutter that worked for the company. In 1971, a great opportunity presented itself. Safeway was going to centralize their meat processing at a plant in Vernon, California. This was very close to south-central Los Angeles. Vernon was famous for meat plants including Farmer John meats and Union Meat Packing, which actually had a kill floor. Safeway's meat plant was to be a state of the art facility. Over 2000 hind quarters and fore quarters of beef would be split on two giant bull saws. Two smaller band saws would finish breaking the beef into smaller cuts. There were two conveyor belts, one for each line, that were about 80 feet long. The deboned finished product went to a cryo-vac area. There they would be bagged with a special machine that sucked all the air out of the bag. This was done to give the meat a longer and fresher shelf life. Altogether, there were about 150 meat cutters on the boning lines. To say that the Safeway meat plant was a rough place to work at would be an understatement, for sure. Many people don't realize that in the late 60s and early 70s our country had a man shortage due to the Vietnam War. Add to that the fact that demand for beef was significantly increased due to the military's need for meat products. The company faced tremendous production challenges and the workers paid the price.

I was still working at the Safeway stores as a retail meat cutter in West Covina, California. My duties consisted of working every night and weekends. At the Vernon meat plant the work hours were 8 AM to 5 PM, Monday through Friday, with weekends off. The problem was the environment. Truck drivers that picked up meat at the plant and then delivered to our stores were always telling wild stories about what went on at the meat plant. It was really a perfect storm for drugs and violence. Approximately 25% of the plant workforce had been trained in prison due to the countries man shortage. Another 25% were veterans coming back from Vietnam. The real meat boners were older guys that had worked in wholesale breaking plants all their lives. Because of the rough and mean environment, most retail meat cutters did not want to venture into what some referred to as the "insane asylum." Working days and having their weekends off was not enough to lure them. I wanted to be with my little family so I transferred and became a journeyman meat boner.

My first day at the Vernon meat plant was quite a culture shock. We were supposed to start work at 8 AM sharp so I arrived at 7 AM to get a feel for what I had gotten myself into. The plant was a huge gray concrete building that had no windows of any kind, surrounded by 10 foot chain-link fence with razor wire on top. My first thought was this is a prison! An armed security guard stood at the entrance and had everyone open their lunch pails when entering the plant and when leaving. The loading dock was full of trucks with workers unloading hundreds of hind and forequarter's of beef. When I presented myself at the front office they gave me a white smock, a mesh glove, and a leather belly guard. Since I was going to be boning beef all day the potential for severe cuts was great. This was protective gear. Not only was I going to be working with razor sharp knives but I also had a meat hook to stab and control the cuts of beef. That meat hook became an extension of my left hand and even today 42 years later I have a callous between my two fingers from which the hook protruded. I was also given a green plastic safety helmet to signal that I was a worker. Management wore white helmets. The environment certainly made me feel out of place. Being only 21 years old and still baby faced didn't help.

Inside the meat plant it was cold and very wet. It matched some of the personalities I ran into. My first day, wanting to be cordial, I went up to this big black fellow who was standing alone. I tried to introduce myself. He looked at my outstretched hand with contempt and said "I can't talk to you, get away." I later learned that, Big Al, as he was called, had been trained in prison where segregation is practiced on a daily basis.

The older meat boners took a liking to me because I was respectful and polite to them. This turned out to be a real blessing, since they took special interest and taught me many of their secrets when it came to boning. They would call me "kid" since the older guys were in their late 50s or early 60s. A weird metamorphosis would happen to people that went to work in the meat plant. It was amazing to see grown men act worse than high school kids. Their language became totally perverse. They no longer referred to themselves by name. Instead, they would call each other "M-F'ers", "shit head," or even worse. The troubling part for me was the party they were calling out to would always answer, "Yes, are you calling me?" Drugs were rampant throughout the plant. Every morning you were offered "black beauties" or "whites," these were amphetamine pills to get through the day. The majority of the guys would have hangovers from the night before. Still, in this environment I tried to not become twisted. You can't help but be influenced to a certain degree but you must set boundaries. What made me strong was having clarity of why I was there. My little family, Eunice and my two daughters, Leticia and Marisela, depended on me. That was all I needed to know. Besides the older guys were my friends. No matter what, they were not as crazy and vulgar as the younger guys that had been trained in prison or just back from Vietnam.

One of the older men I admired and respected was Henry Soto. Henry was in his late fifties or early 60s. In spite of having worked over 40 years in the meat plant dungeons of Vernon, he still walked with his shoulders back and erect. He always had a witty smile. He was what we would call in Spanish a "huero," which means light skinned. Behind his wrinkled face you could see his dark blue eyes. It was Henry who began calling me "kid". Henry Soto taught me everything he knew about breaking beef and boning. I really looked up to him as a mentor. After about a year at the Safeway meat plant, I had established myself as one of the best boners. My specialty was boning fore shanks, which is the front forearm of the steer. The skin and meat is especially tough and you need a razor-sharp knife and perfect hook control in order to leave the shank bone white after removing all the muscle. I learned to completely bone a fore shank in 11 to 15 seconds. I had become number one, the fastest meat boner on the line. This made me proud and almost everyone respected me, thanks to Henry's kindness and willingness to take the time to teach me. It felt great to get home to my wife and two baby daughters and have dinner with them knowing I was a good provider.

One day, Henry Soto told me, "Kid, we want you to become one of the guys." I said, "Thanks Henry." He continued, "This Friday after work we're going to get together and have some beers. We want you to come. I have something special lined up for you and it's a really good looking huera (blonde) that you can have some fun with." About five of the old guys were standing around us. If there is such a thing as an awkward moment, this was super awkward. Henry and the guys felt they were doing me a great favor almost like an initiation of sorts. I broke the lengthy awkward silence and said, "Thanks Henry but I have to get home to my wife and two daughters Friday evening." A couple of seconds later, which seemed like an eternity, an uproar of laughter that I'm sure was heard throughout the entire plant spontaneously erupted. "The kid is pussy whipped guys," my friend and mentor said while turning and looking at each of the guys as they began to laugh even harder. "Come on kid. Have some fun. Look at this," Henry said as he showed me a photograph of a blonde young lady perhaps in her late 20s. She was stark naked showing off her ample behind and at the same time facing backwards with a truly Jezebel smile. I exhaled, swallowed, and said, "I'm sorry but I really need to get home." The guys all walked away laughing and shaking their heads. It was hard for me to assess my feelings at that moment. My stance was not a self-righteous one because I was not judging or condemning anything they did. What I was sure of was that I had to have a private conversation with Henry Soto while the feelings were still fresh. So at the end of the day, I approached Henry in front of our lockers and I waited until we were alone. I approached the subject very respectfully, "Henry may I have a word with you?" Henry immediately said "Sure kid, what's up?" I was being as sincere as I could and said, "You know when we were talking in front of the guys it really hurt when you laughed at me probably because I have so much respect and admiration for you. You're my mentor." Henry was a little surprised that I was approaching the matter with such resolve, he replied, "Kid, don't worry about it that's the way we guys are. You're doing the right thing by going home to your family." BINGO! Henry understood! In my inexperience I said, "Thanks Henry. You know when I get home from work my two little girls wrap themselves around my legs and yell BIG DADDY IS HOME, I love that feeling."

Once again, being naïve, I asked Henry if he had children of his own. My reasoning was that Henry probably really loved his kids. Here was probably some common ground that we could both relate to. "Thank you for understanding Henry. I'm sure you love your family to. How many children do you have?" Henry quickly said "Never mind kid. I don't talk about my family here at work." Now my curiosity was running wild. "Tell me Henry, how many children do you have and what are their ages? I'm your friend." Nothing could have prepared me for his next answer, "NINETEEN! I have 19 children. I have been married five times." I did not intend to but "OH NO!" came out of my open mouth. "Henry, I can't imagine how much pain being married five times has caused you. All I want is my little family, my wife and two little daughters, that's all." "Kid you're doing the right thing. I told you there's nothing like your first family," Henry said. He understood and that was a big relief. Then he said, "Kid, promise me that you will not embarrass me in front of the guys and I promise not to tease you ever again."

THOUGHTS

Without being self-righteous, to me it is sad and tragic the pain we can inflict on our loved ones. In my opinion, real men should be Protectors of their family not the Destroyers. When people reach their final destination we all look back at the lives we have lived. One foolish and selfish act can tarnish a lifetime of good deeds.

Who needs the drama and pain? Learn to be content with your own blessings. My daughter, Marisela, has a very truthful and interesting saying it goes something like this, "Some men think the grass is greener on the other side. Maybe if you take better care of your grass and water it more it will be green and beautiful." AMEN

I Regret the Way I Lived My Life

These haunting words still resonate in my mind even though they were spoken over 30 years ago. It was my own father who exhaled these words over and over again, every day, for over a year. He was literally on his deathbed with terminal stomach cancer. It truly was a pitiful sight to see his emaciated living corpse laying there. No longer was the mean, 250 pound man, who always seemed to be looking for an argument, able to take care of even himself. Now he was a mere 70 pounds of bone, covered with a layer of yellow colored skin that looked like leather. "I regret the way I live my life." Every day he would make this sad confession to himself. How impotent and sad he must have felt, not even being able to walk or barely talk. I had great pity for him. After all, he was my father. My poor mother was his nurse, 24/7. She had aged 20 years in just one year, that's what it looked like to me. My father was only 62 years old and my poor mother 54. She was his nurse, never leaving his side. My mother was the noble wife and she never complained. She was as beautiful inside as she was on the outside. Many times I would think to myself that my mother was much too good for my father. He would constantly belittle her in public and was physically abusive when he would get drunk in his younger years, and that was often.

I remember being a child in the 1950s when he would always promise to take my brothers, sisters, and I to fun places like Disneyland or fishing. He promised this hundreds of times and hundreds of times he would break his promise. He didn't have time for his children but always made time to go to bars and get drunk. Even at my wedding reception in December of 1967, he ended up in a fist fight with my older brother-in-law, who was as crazy as him. It didn't matter that it was supposed to be a sacred occasion. This very special event belonged to Eunice and I and he made it about him. I believe that in life there are good examples and bad examples. Truth is that we can learn from both of them. My dad was a bad example. I vowed before heaven and earth not to be like him. My position was confirmed on his deathbed. Over and over again he said, "I regret the way I lived my life." Of course, I felt very sad for him as he lay on his bed with no way to feel comfortable. The cancerous tumors in his stomach had surfaced and broken through his skin. They would rupture and expose what seemed like many little tumors filled with blood mixed with pus. The stench my mother had to endure when cleaning them was awful.

The day my father died is engraved in my mind. He died on April 13, 1981. Since then I've come to the conclusion that he was a very ill individual. Two years of fighting in World War II in the South Pacific didn't help. As a matter of fact, he was severely wounded in the campaign to recapture the Solomon Islands. I believe my dad had post-traumatic syndrome, before it was diagnosed as a real condition that soldiers in combat suffer from. Whatever the reasons for his behavior, they were no matter what, his choices. The outcome was the same and he left everybody in his family shell shocked. When he died that April day of 1981, I learned two very valuable lessons. First, time races past us very rapidly and it seems like before we know it, we get old. The second lesson is that no matter how dominant a person is in our life, when they die, everything keeps going. Personal choice is our responsibility, nobody else's. For good or for bad we are the architects of our own destiny. My choice, when I come to the end of my days, is not to drown in regret and have to have to say, "I regret the way I lived my life."

THOUGHTS

It is not easy for me to write negative things about my father but it is the truth and my mother has verified it. We are all the sum total of our choices and experiences. It is within our power to choose to be a victim and continue to victimize our own loved ones. A better choice is to break the mold and this too is within our power. We all have a day of reckoning and the end of the matter is what is important. How will we be remembered? Better yet, how will we remember ourselves? It is our choice.

Trees Die at the Top

When I was 15 years old, attending El Monte high school in California, I wanted to play football. The thought of playing running back was pretty exciting. Mr. Langley, the football coach was impressed because I was the fastest runner on the freshman team. At practice I excelled and could hardly wait to get my helmet and football uniform. Coach told me that I would be the starting running back. First, I would have to pass the football physical administered by a doctor the school contracted with. I stood in line with about 20 other high school kids in my underwear and waited my turn. The doctor took out his stethoscope and listened intently to my heart. It seemed like he was taking longer listening to my heart than he did with the other boys. He took off his stethoscope and leaned back in his chair and said, "You have a heart murmur young man. I cannot pass you until you get a clearance from a cardiologist." He suggested I visit White Memorial Hospital in Los Angeles. The doctor then gave me a note that explained his findings and opinion for me to take to my parents. That night, I showed my parents the doctor's note and told them what he said. Within two days we were at the White Memorial Hospital waiting room. They called us in and were greeted by the cardiologist. White Memorial Hospital was a training hospital then. Instead of being taken into a single room we found ourselves in the middle of a mini medical arena. I was placed on a hospital bed and the cardiologist proceeded with a battery of tests and examinations. All the while, on the second floor, looking down were about 20 interns as the head cardiologist explained every procedure and finding. The exam took about one hour. They asked us to please go to the waiting room while the cardiologist and the interns conferred. My mother, father and I waited about an hour and then the doctors appeared.

There were about five of them including the cardiologist. "He definitely has a heart murmur and it sounds like one of his heart valves is leaking. Did he have rheumatic fever as a child? Even though my mother was not proficient in English she understood and answered, "Si, el tuvo fiebre rumatica de chico," confirming the doctors suspicion. It felt like my world came crashing down on me when the doctor said, "I believe he is going to need open heart surgery to repair that leaking heart valve," so matter of fact. My shocked parents hesitated and said they wanted a second opinion before making such a serious decision. The doctor was visibly angered and rather rudely stated, "It is my opinion that if he doesn't have open heart surgery, it's possible he won't live past 21 years." Now my heart really sank. I actually experienced some pain in my chest. That meant I might not be able to get a driver's license because I could drop dead at any moment.

When I returned to El Monte high school, they placed me in a special education class with other kids suffering from a variety of illnesses and limitations. One kid, I still remember his name, Jeff, had open-heart surgery a year before. When he would take off his shirt, you could see a prominent fifteen inch scar that extended one inch below his Adam's apple to just above his naval. Holy cow! That's what I'm going to look like, I remember telling myself. The mind is very powerful and it can certainly play tricks on you. I really felt like I was dying and it seemed that I was getting weaker every day. Everything seemed potentially dangerous to me. The doctor's words, "He probably won't live to be 21 years old," haunted me continuously.

Finally, we went for the second medical opinion at USC Medical Hospital in Los Angeles. We also knew it as the General Hospital. Similar tests were performed by nurses and a cardiologist. I was expecting more bad news after the tests were complete. This time the doctor came out to talk with us by himself and not in a group. I remember listening intently as he began to speak. I was expecting the worst. "He definitely has a heart murmur but I think it's functional," The doctor said. He continued, "Some young people develop these heart murmurs and eventually out grow them. It is my professional opinion that open heart surgery would be too traumatic and intrusive at this time because there is a chance that he can function just fine with it." I broke out in a huge smile and it seemed like the weight of the world had been lifted from my shoulders. Perhaps I said it out loud but I do remember thinking "Hallelujah, thank you God. I'm not going to die." I went from feeling sickly and weak back to the athlete playing football and baseball and in regular PE class. I never gave my heart murmur a second thought. As a matter of fact, I played varsity third-base four years and was captain of the baseball team my junior and senior years.

Now I am almost 63 years old. I can still make myself remember how my mind had convinced me that I would not live past 21 years old. I was already convinced that I would die, not live. That's when I realized that trees die at the top. This is an old proverb that is so true. Actually trees do die at the top because the fungus or disease attacks them at the top. Sometimes the trees die at the top because they cannot adapt to certain elements or environment. Throughout my life that experience has taught me that while we have life, there is hope. Health is really our true wealth.

THOUGHTS

Remember this saying, "Life is fair… it beats everybody up." We are all confronted with powerful challenges and sometimes they are life-threatening. Why is it that some people with identical cancers live long lives and some die shortly after being diagnosed? That is a very sensitive question but one for the ages. One survivor told me that when she was told about her breast cancer she was determined not to let the cancer destroy her life. She said, "I may have cancer but I will not become my cancer."

When I was diagnosed with my heart murmur in 1964 at 15 years old it almost killed me. Not because I was in danger of dying from my heart ailment. The mistake I made was to become my perceived heart condition. I accepted what the first doctor said as gospel. Throughout my life I have learned never to give up my thinking ability and get second opinions when it comes to serious medical issues. Never allow negativity or self-imposed limitations to consume you. It is factually true, "Trees die at the top," and some people do too. We all have CHOICE and we could choose to not die at the top but rather to "live at the top", choose life.

The Story of the Beautiful Giant Dahlia

When my family moved to Victorville California I became interested in planting and growing flowers. I had always heard of the beautiful national flower of Mexico known as the Dahlia. They truly are majestic and come in many different colors. Their colors range from deep purple, to bright yellow, and some which are known as dinner plate Dahlias because of their impressive size have white tips. Dahlias grow from bulbs that you plant in the soil. They are perennials which mean they will come back every year.

My worry was that the winters were too cold in Victorville to allow dahlias to flourish. My bulbs went into the ground in winter and in spring one dominant dahlia plant sprouted. It began to grow rapidly because the spring weather was perfect. Every day I would measure its growth and health until one day the miracle happened. A beautiful purple dahlia with white tips was born. It was gorgeous and was the first dahlia I had ever grown.

My plan was to show the entire family this enchanting flower the next day when it would fully bloom and its actual size would be that of a dinner plate. That evening I went out to the planter and much to my shock, IT WAS GONE! I felt my anger begin to flush my face and I had to know, who would have picked my beautiful dahlia without my permission?

In those days our daughters and their families were our neighbors. Four houses adjacent to each other with the backyard fences removed so our grandchildren could all play together.

My first neighbor was my daughter Marisela. I knocked on her back door and announced, "Its dad. Can I come in?" Marisela answered, "Sure dad. Come on in. Do you want anything to drink?" I said, "thank you but it's okay. What I'm really trying to find out is who cut my dahlia?" I asked in a frustrated tone. "No I haven't seen anything. What is a dahlia?" I explained that it is a beautiful large flower and this one was especially beautiful because of its deep purple color with white tips. "No dad. I can't help you but maybe Elena knows who took your dahlia."

I went to Elena's house and repeated the same inquiry. By this time I was really starting to get irritated. Elena answered the same as Marisela. She recommended that I go next door to my eldest daughter Leticia's house.

I was mumbling to myself as I walked the 50 feet to my eldest daughter's back sliding door. I knocked on the door and my daughter saw it was me. "Come in dad," she welcomed. Leticia had a big smile on her face and said before I could continue my investigation, "Look at the beautiful flower baby John picked for me. He said the flower was beautiful like his mother and that he loved me so much that he wanted me to have it. Isn't that nice?"

My heart melted. My two-year-old grandson was the little culprit that picked the giant dahlia. My daughter, Leticia, had placed the beautiful dahlia in a vase with water. It was really much more beautiful now in its new home than it was in the planter with nobody except me even noticing it.

What baby John did was a very loving act to please his mom and now the dahlia had accomplished a greater purpose. All I could say was, "Wow! That is so wonderful Mija." Over the years, I have seen dozens of dahlias grow in my many gardens. It is amazing to me that even today almost 15 years later, the one dahlia that I will never forget is the one baby John picked and gave to his mom.

THOUGHTS

It is wonderful to see our young children do acts of pure love. Baby John's intent was superior to anything that I could've done with that beautiful dahlia. Sometimes our busy lifestyles can cause us to forget the greatest blessing of all, our children. It is important to cultivate and reinforce their good feelings and acts. The only thing baby John wanted was his mother's approval and that's as pure as it gets.

We as adults have a responsibility to influence in a positive way their heart condition. That is an incredible power bestowed upon us as parents. There is so much we can learn from the unselfish acts of younger children.

Memories and Reflections on Raising Daughters

So many times I have heard people say that it is much easier to raise sons than daughters. I wouldn't know. I never had sons. To me it would be very difficult to understand a greater joy than raising my four daughters. Sometimes I am moved to write letters to myself about being a father of our four daughters. This is one of those letters.

The most challenging and rewarding experience in my life has been raising my four daughters. I can only speak from my personal experience regarding this matter. When they were born they were brought home to a very loving environment prepared by their awesome mother. Just like seedlings our babies required special care.

Their mother, Eunice, watched over and nursed them like a mother hawk watches its newborn chicks. Every need they might have had was attended to and they were never neglected. As they began to grow, just like the plants in our garden, other challenges made themselves manifest, battling weeds. These weeds are very resilient and determined to harm or corrupt your plants. You have to protect your plants from these weeds because they are relentless. Sometimes you can't identify the weeds until it is almost too late.

When we were raising our daughters I never forgot the principle that bad associations spoil good habits! Some kids that come into your children's lives are exactly like the weeds I describe. When I was raising my teenage daughters I realized that my job was not a popularity contest. That was fine. My four daughters are the pride of my life. They are now grown and have families of their own.

My eldest daughter, Leticia, is forty three years old. My second daughter, Marisela, is forty two and Elena is forty. Our baby Gina is thirty seven years old. It could be said that I am very prejudice, but this is a father's prerogative. To me they are the greatest women in the world. One day I had the privilege of sitting at our dinner table and listening to a conversation they were having amongst each other. We raised our daughters to be very opinionated and honest. I was compelled to write a letter for them to read.

Conclusion

MY DEAREST DAUGHTERS

12/26/2011

I was compelled to write this letter with the intent of persuading all of you of how proud I am of each and every one of you.

At Gina and Jason's 19th wedding anniversary, held at my daughter Leticia's house, a spiritual epiphany happened to me. I listened to my women discuss such profound subjects as fate and the many ironies of life. My heart was warmed and I realized in my soul what great daughters I have had the privilege of influencing. It was humbling because it was the answer to many of my personal and intimate prayers.

There were no arguments but so many different opinions, all intelligent. Respect and love ruled the night's conversation and you all treated each other as the women of substance that you are. It was a privilege to be amongst you, my daughters.

The little village that mom and I started with no plan or guiding star except love has flourished. In a little bit of a melancholy way, I recognize and praise that the village is now composed of strong little tribes. I say melancholy in the sense of mixed emotions. No regrets, but it does mark a changing of the guard which is both good and necessary.

Jaime Alvarez

In life, the children become the parents, the parents become grandparents, and eventually grandparents become great grandparents. This privilege is neither by default nor entitlement it is earned by devotion. I can truly say for mom and me that we devoted our lives to our four daughters and you responded by giving us the greatest gift of all, family and grandchildren.

You are all so intelligent and mature with wisdom and each of you have your own special journey. It is now your turn to be mothers and soon possibly grandmothers. I can only praise Almighty God with eternal thanks and embrace this beautiful reality and recognize that this is the way it should be.

Your father.

12/26/2011

Left to Right,
Elena Labastida, Gina Bosch, Marisela Labastida, Leticia Eastland

When wisdom enters into your heart and knowledge itself becomes pleasant to your very soul, thinking ability itself will keep guard over you, discernment itself will safeguard you, to deliver you from the bad way, from the man speaking perverse things, from those leaving the paths of uprightness to walk in the ways of darkness. —

Proverbs 2:10-13

Open Invitation

It is amazing how our lives can be molded by wise sayings. Throughout history every Society has developed their own "dichos" in order to guide them.

After reading "The Collective Works of Jaime Alvarez featuring Dichos de Mi Madre," I personally invite you to share your wise sayings via Facebook. Visit my Facebook page at http://www.facebook.com/**jaimealvarezwisdom**. I will also accept your sayings via email at jalvarez1949@aol.com. With your permission the "dichos" or "sayings" will be shared with my friends and will possibly be featured as a different saying every week on Facebook. So let's make your life delicious and share wisdom.

In the future I will make myself available by conducting seminars in English and Spanish to help first time book writers overcome obstacles that may be preventing them from publishing their first book. Remember everybody has something interesting to say and at least one book to write.

Your Own Dichos and Sayings

NOTES:

_____

_____

_____

_____

_____

_____

_____

_____

_____

_____

_____

_____

_____

_____

Your Own Dichos and Sayings

NOTES:

_____

_____

_____

_____

_____

_____

_____

_____

_____

_____

_____

_____

_____

Your Own Dichos and Sayings

NOTES:

_____

_____

_____

_____

_____

_____

_____

_____

_____

_____

_____

_____

_____

Your Own Dichos and Sayings

NOTES:

_____

_____

_____

_____

_____

_____

_____

_____

_____

_____

_____

_____

_____